Untameable City

Untameable City

Poems on the Nature of Houston

Edited by Sandi Stromberg

Mutabilis Press
Houston

© Copyright 2015 Mutabilis Press

Individual poems and photographs copyright by the authors and photographers, and used with permission.

All rights reserved by the authors and photographers.

Photo credits:

Mike Alexander, page 59
Carolyn Tourney Florek, page 83
Bob Florek, page 117
Priscilla Frake, page 47
Isabelle Perreau, pages 25, 37, 71, 143
Betsy Siegel, page 131
Varsha Saraiya-Shah, page 105
Heidi Straube, pages 13, 95

Cover art by Carolyn Tourney Florek

ISBN number 978-0-9729432-9-1

Library of Congress Control Number: 2015913494

www.mutabilispress.org

Foreword

It has been ten years since Mutabilis Press published *TimeSlice*, our first anthology collecting the work of Houston poets. In some ways it is remarkable that ten years later Mutabilis Press is at it again, taking on the task of appealing to our community of poets for their poems that reflect the very nature of Houston, a city in constant flow and growth, a place bigger and more poetry-packed than ever before. I have observed many times in conversation with poet friends that there are so many poetry events in Houston that it is impossible to attend them all. The artist's dilemma is time itself. We constantly balance our desire to be part of the greater community with finding the time necessary to write our poems.

Untameable City: Poems on the Nature of Houston, bringing together the work of eighty-three poets, is evidence that time, serious time, is being devoted to the craft. As publisher and managing editor, I am impressed, grateful, and best of all, enriched by the poetry and the poets gathered into our new anthology.

A collection like this just doesn't materialize. As in the writing of a poem, the making of an anthology is an arduous collective process. Mutabilis Press would not have had a ten-year run of publishing poetry if there hadn't been a selfless team of individuals behind the scenes, working very hard at all aspects of editing and publishing. With *Untameable City*, Sandi Stromberg came on board and accepted the challenge and responsibility of editorship. Working with Sandi has been pure joy—a true collaboration with Sandi and the other board members of Mutabilis Press: Mike Alexander, Kristi Beer, Stan Crawford, Carolyn Dahl, Priscilla Frake, Varsha Shah, and Rebecca Spears, and the technical support of Bob Florek. Their talents and dedication combined are present here, realized as *Untameable City*.

Houston Poets, thank you, thank you. Here is your book.

—*Carolyn Tourney Florek*

Contents

Foreword	5
Introduction	11
Carolyn Adams	14
James Adams	15
Mike Alexander	16
Michael Baldwin	18
Joe Barnes	19
David A. Bart	20
Kristi Beer	21
Paula Beltrán	22
Michael Berryhill	26
Ann Reisfeld Boutté	27
Barbara Ann Carle	28
kathleen cook	29
Sara Cooper	30
Sarah Cortez	31
Kay L. Cox	32
Stan Crawford	33
Carolyn Dahl	34
Robin Davidson	35
Margo Davis	38
Diane DeGaetani	39
Winston Derden	40
Carolyn Tourney Florek	41
Dede Fox	42
Priscilla Frake	44
Adamarie Fuller	45
Jeannie Gambill	48

Elisa A. Garza	49
John Gorman	51
Maryann Gremillion	52
William Guest	53
Laura Quinn Guidry	56
Marian Haddad	60
Jerry Hamby	62
Michelle Hartman	63
Bradley Earle Hoge	64
Adam Holt	66
Cindy Huyser	69
Angélique Jamail	72
Joshua C. Jones	74
Claire Kageyama-Ramakrishnan	75
Laurence V. Kelly	77
Jim LaVilla-Havelin	78
Catherine Lee	79
Thad Logan	80
Janet Lowery	84
Anne Robinson Mabry	86
Dodie Messer Meeks	87
John Milkereit	88
Terry Jude Miller	90
Jane E. Mulholland	91
Mark Stephen Mullee	93
Carol Louise Munn	96
Sheryl L. Nelms	97
Stella Nesanovich	99
David Olson	100
Trilla Pando	101
Mary Parham	102

Richard H. Peake	103
Donna E. Perkins	106
Elina Petrova	107
Dustin Pickering	109
henry 7. reneau, jr.	110
Lynn C. Reynolds	111
Sally Ridgway	112
Gary S. Rosin	113
Varsha Saraiya-Shah	114
Jenna Pashley Smith	118
Loueva Smith	119
Rebecca A. Spears	120
Sandi Stromberg	122
Larry D. Thomas	124
Nancy Thorleifson	125
Margo Stutts Toombs	126
Elizabeth Tornes	127
William Turner	129
Evangelina Vigil	132
Randall Watson	134
Weasel	135
Chuck Wemple	136
Scott Wiggerman	137
Steve Wilson	138
S.L. Wisenberg	139
Vanessa Zimmer-Powell	140
Biographies	145

Introduction

When I left the Netherlands for Houston twenty-three years ago, I braced to live in a desert. Yet, as the plane grew closer and I was told to buckle my seat belt, what I saw spreading below was "A tapestry / Eight shades of green," as Dodie Messer Meeks describes it in her poem, "Green."

In Houston's urban sprawl—unzoned and seemingly uncontained—I found contradictions: a mixture of Wild West and cosmopolitan sophistication, a cultured and civilized city coexisting with Mother Nature and her wildness.

How could it be otherwise in a place founded by two entrepreneurial brothers in 1836 on the shores of one swampy bayou and crisscrossed by three others? (See William Guest's "Deliver This Letter" for the story.)

This is a city where possums and skunks walk the streets, alligators surface during floods, and raccoons do their thievery in the night. Yet by day, Houston rules the lucrative oil and energy trade, boasts the world's largest medical center, and is home to NASA.

All this is fodder for the thriving community of poets and this anthology. What better way to celebrate a city's diversity, its multiplicity than through strong images, painted in words across a broad canvas. In this collection, eighty-three poets raise their voices to sing, in the best Greek tradition, "Oh Houston, You Untameable City!"

****

While we want much from the city, the question arises: *What does Houston want from us?*

"The city wants its story, its genius or spirit, to be recognized and remembered through fantasy and imagination, not just through ascending growth and rationalistic planning," says Ronald Schenk, Ph.D., Jungian analyst. "It wants to be reflected upon through pools and runways of water, not just literalized, narcissistic reflections of glass buildings. It wants its darkness seen, not just its sparkle. It wants its depth penetrated, not simply its sprawl and its heights to be extended ... the city wants to be continuously re-dis-covered and re-imagined. In this mode, the poets of our tradition have blazed a trail."*

Indeed, the poets, whose poems appear here, invite us to travel their varied trails with its potholes, weeds, and construction, to sit in its traffic jams, to swelter in its heat and humidity. They zoom in on the javelinas and fire ants, the bayous and pollution; the great art, pop art, and art car parade; the mixed neighborhoods, ethnicities, and the homeless; the hurricanes and their threats; the bountiful music, theatre, and dance.

Not New York City. Not Los Angeles. Not Chicago.

Houston's opposites persevere. Sophistication and wildness unite. Grackles, flamingoes, and live oaks enjoy the sky along with refineries and skyscrapers. Palmettos peek through cracks in miles of concrete, bats flit among morning glories. An owl screeches in the night, a copperhead slithers through the garden, and rabbits multiply.

Behold Houston, America's fourth largest city ... untameable.

—*Sandi Stromberg*

* From the lecture, "City and Soul," given at The Jung Center in Houston, Thursday, May 14, 2015.

Carolyn Adams

Weeds

I photograph them
in the mornings,
these precise little flowers
and their microscopic foliage,
growing wild
in the leaf clutter of my yard.

They're best in the morning.
Too much attention from the sun,
and they close up like secrets.

Butter yellow, salmon pink,
soft lilac, pale sky blue.

Slipper-shaped.
Five perfect petals,
pin-wheeled.
A bell on a slender stalk.

Assigned such small tasks,
they carry on business almost invisibly.
A shoe tap could destroy them.
Raindrops are catastrophic.

Years ago, I'd mow them
over. Pull them out by roots.
Now, I sit with them
in early light,
before a clumsy foot
disturbs their industry.

Before it rains.
Before the summer sends them away.

James Adams

Raccoon Pears

Summer eventide (with fruit), Buffalo Bayou

Four tunes, playing black-grey
and white—eat carefully
in this backdoor flood light:

One nervous, flitting her fluted
tale, ringed about in muted stripe—
lashing a tongue to a snail.

Two impervious, washing four wicked
paws, over-fooded and tight—
splashing green gum in two jaws.

Three a dance number, splitting his footed
spats, monk-eyed, hand-ready and ripe—
dashing the verdant skinned batt.

Four waltzes, coattails, fur and mask;
trundlers, arched-back into the night,
caching their mashed-fruited bundles.

Mike Alexander

Damage Tour

i

The dark sky howls.
    We bar the doors
with sodden towels,
    & sop the floors.
The sea wall roars;
    our radio tells
the size of swells
    on Galveston.
Our power's gone.

The radio squalls.
    Eyewitness News
is taking calls,
    but blows a fuse,
so that we lose
    what words we had
to say how bad
    the damage was.
Dead static buzz.

Inside, we drain
    our batteries,
while gusts of rain
    uproot the trees,
like storming seas
    or a raging tide.
The eye outside
    refuses sleep.
Our ceilings weep.

ii

Daylight brings us the tallies, gulf communities
   destroyed, houses blown out to sea, bridges collapsed,
boats thrown from the marina like discarded toys,
   extensive flooding—no one thought to build an ark—
the eastern windows of the ziggurats downtown,
   all broken, sidewalk given teeth of shattered glass…

Our shredded yard is spackled with confetti'd leaves,
   our sewer clotted with debris, our street a moat;
one local wades across in rubber boots to say
   when the transformer blew, a well-known restaurant
five blocks from us caught fire & burned down to the brick.
   He's taking out his children on a damage tour.

A dead live oak has crashed across a neighbor's porch,
   his daughter scrambles through its branches like a squirrel;
meanwhile, his second-story deck has fallen in,
   suspended now above twin phone & cable lines—
I help him rope & lift it clear, to break it up
   & throw the pieces down. It crashes to the ground.

We got off easy. Still, the ticking orison
   of water dripping into cooking pans we've set
around the house tells as much truth as any clock.
   Our ceilings still might fall. We've lost our Internet.
Our cats sprawled on the floor stare up at us in shock.
   We pack our babies in their carriers, & run.

Michael Baldwin

Leaf Laughter

Elms
        and oaks
                and tupelos
unleaving,
        ungrieving,
                undressing
tree tresses, confessing
        with colors their
                seasonal sin.
Leaf laughter
        comes after
                quitting their day jobs.
Dancing while dying,
        the leaves keep on trying,
                seducing the wind,
their ramble
        and scramble
                and gambol extend.
We without winter
        fill five months
                with Autumn.
For leaves that's a lifetime
        they would not
                rescind.

Joe Barnes

A Corner in Montrose

The window is gone, the store behind it gutted,
but a sign still swings to the traffic's pulse.
"Est. 1987" it reads simply but in endearing pride,
a date that might be yesterday in European cities
or even in their Boston-New York-Philly brethren,
but here evokes a time so remote it conjures up
the horse and buggy. A barbershop? A bakery?
I probably drove past the place a thousand times
and never knew. I won't know now.

Already the bulldozers assemble to raze
whatever it was and squads of hardhats
rendezvous to raise whatever will be next:
A vertiginous alp of condos, its cliffs inlaid
with lozenges of soft, expensive light?
Or a neo-classical mall of cast-concrete plinths
and caryatids slipped from silicon molds?
Someplace, surely, where I won't be rich
enough to shop or rent or, God help me, even park.

There is a species of immortality
among the block-long excavations and towers rising,
exultant, behind their filigree of scaffold,
where today never lingers long enough to form a proper past.

What the aging world calls history—those strata
of brick and stone that bear the human weight
of earned lives and livelihoods—here is merely rubble
to be trucked away. Only we grow old.

David A. Bart

In the Wilderness

Now he's done it,
that bellowing man has furiously knocked
all the single serving sugar packets
off his table, an ever-so-slight mess
that the food court avoids like vomit.

He's face down, crying on the table
and he's really, really sorry,
explaining himself to someone
no one else can see.
Now he's up and ambling

in two worlds at once
with open fly and loud pronouncements
that break the smooth effluence
of the Galleria drudges.
The rage of his witness summons

three novice security guys
who make way for him
to a glittering park of cars,
the lot of the split-brained seer
whose mouthful of expletives
spills out like grasshoppers and honey.

Kristi Beer

Before the Hurricane

We all scurry like ants
before the fall of a foot—
I nab an errant bottle of water
misplaced among the popcorn
like a hidden treasure,
a jar of generic peanut butter,
canned green beans.

But the man in front of me
puts Schweppes and brie and biscotti
on the grocery counter,
then reaches over
and plucks a bouquet
of yellow tiger lilies,
puts them to his nose,
inhales once
and adds them to his pile
of essential supplies.

Paula Beltrán

Primer Día: Advice To A Greenhorn

You name your lawn mowing business "Smith and Sons" even if your name is Gomez, because "Smith" gets more calls than "Gomez." You drive down South Shepherd in Houston to maneuver your double cab red Chevy and the trailer full of equipment worth more than you'll ever be worth on your way to wide oak-lined streets. You place both your hands on the steering wheel so that the people in the next lane see that you are responsible. You sometimes steer your truck with only three fingers, leaning your left elbow on the window frame to let some men—and some women—know the truck and the business are yours.

Tuesdays and Thursdays are how often you drive with the windows down so that you don't forget just how recent it was that you were able to afford the new truck. Mondays are when you let the crew ride with you in the cab so they can forget for a moment that the equipment in the trailer is worth more than they ever will be. Wednesdays are when you buy everybody lunch because it's the day for the "green" homes and you charge more for using organic grass seeds and propane over gas because it's good business and your son—whom you've never let ride in the truck inside or outside—told you you should care about the size of your shoe on the planet.

You turn left slowly onto Inwood Drive where the lady with the shapely *chamorros* sits outside picture-reading to the three year old she cares for while imagining her own kids back home playing in the surf of Playa de Roatán. This is how you park in front of Dr. __'s house and—are you paying attention—this is me reminding you and the rest of the crew not to speak Spanish. This is how you say good morning Mrs. __ in English, and this is how you stop to smile and how you say it's a beautiful day, Mrs. __ (practice!) before going back to your work if she walks up to you again. This is how you smile when the heat makes you forget and she hears you cursing the fire ants and the brown patches of dog piss messing last month's re-seeding and she waves her hand with that ring you assume is a fake and asks why are you speaking in Spanish when you're in America? This is how you wait to see her retreat into the cool of her home swinging her hips in white cotton so thin you imagine she wears them only for you.

This is how you don't speak Spanish even though she's inside and the two o'clock sun seeps through the brown leather of your skin, even if the sharp blades of St. Augustine flying in the air cut again and again through your old bag of English words leaving you with grotesque, mispronounced stumps and at a loss to talk about anything including the tilling, plowing, seeding, mowing, hauling, trimming, mulching, fertilizing you've been doing. Thinking of your son someday learning how to *say* those and all words in Spanish and English is how you get through it. And when you see the competition display stickers of an American flag and the caption "These colors don't run," you buy your own and this is how you place it right above the license plate. Once you've been here fifteen years like me you'll do anything to get out of riding in the trailer with equipment worth more than you'll ever be.

Michael Berryhill

Do This Now

Somewhere in the bamboo thicket by the fence,
a cricket is faintly chirping in the late afternoon.
Listen, I tell Elizabeth, listen, but she wants
more action. She finds a cicada wing floating
in the pool, its iridescent membrane
and veins still intact under one green strut,
all that's left of a summer's droning that began
this morning and died out. Hurricanes are growing
near Africa and menacing us. We throw two
beach balls at each other, light blue and swirled
with what looks like clouds viewed from outer space.
Little earths, I think, little earths. Elizabeth hides
under an air mattress and dares me to hit her with a ball.
Do this now, she insists. Do this now!

Ann Reisfeld Boutté

Terry Hershey Park

That spring day I went cycling
the air was fragrant
with wild jasmine.
Bluebonnets and Indian
paintbrush dotted the slopes
in a purple scarlet patchwork.
Clusters of lavender irises
with black centers
stared back at me.
A squirrel with ebony fur
scampered across the path.
A trio of rabbits, noses twitching,
nibbled native grasses as they
warily eyed passersby.
At Barker Dam,
egrets, like feathered sentries,
patiently surveyed
the flowing waters
for glints of silver.

I rarely see the inside of a
church or synagogue, but
I pedaled home in grace.

Barbara Ann Carle

Flight of the Flamingo

I sip my morning coffee
in my 13th floor nest
up in the sky

A bright pink blur
streaks by my window
Giant black-tipped wings
labor to keep his oval body aloft
long spindly legs trailing
curved neck and beak straining
into the wind

He circles above the trees
in Hermann Park
Is he an escapee from the zoo?
He heads towards the Galleria
a barren place for a water fowl

You knew so much about birds, their habitats
You would love my new glass living room
We could sit on the couch
watch them soar and dive
at eye level
You could teach me all their names

I wish I could pick up the phone and call
Would you be as amazed as I?
Or would you say
He's not rare in Texas, Mom.
He's just lost.

kathleen cook

heedless

we failed to read that cautionary tale,
as busy in our new land, we alchemized
tree, land, and grain, manufactured notes
of green, mighty, but too small to cover
our plundered shame.

each day, in eagerness, we touched
more. the vast continent too small
for us and the buffalo, we nailed them
to our nickels, leveraged those for mansions,
cathedrals, stole the widows' mites.

great forests stood before we came.
rivers had had lives of their own, to rise
and fall, to feed a marsh. we saw
only threat or treasure to gain.
easy the gold, fool's gold.
what we couldn't see before,
we can't not see now:

flattened rainbow of oil on the water
witches plumes of oil gas brew
technology helpless,
pollution apocryphal,

the floor of the sea torn,
the continent sullied,

hapless pelican caught,
our face forever fixed.

Sara Cooper

Where I live

Don't be frightened by the tombstone
manufacturer down the street. She doesn't have you
in mind as she puts hammer to stone, chiseling
each name like a one-word prayer.

Or by our neighbors and their crawfish clan.
Pincerclaws and compound eyes—
they are bottom-feeders, we've heard.

Or by the gator gar with the razor teeth
expelled to the bayou banks after a hard rain,
thrashing in shallow puddles that will disappear
with the risen sun. Or by the man who plays

God after the storm, scouring the shores,
lifting, with gloved hands, each riling fish,
delivering it back to the swim.

Don't be alarmed by the cemetery, gussied up in mylar and silk;
or by the woman's shining face suspended
above her husband's grave like a heart-shaped balloon,
deflating. Or a graveyard flower, steadfast and false.

Or by the bounty the bayou hides—

milk jugs, soda cans, styrofoam cups, inner tubes, trash bags, a dog's
furless leg, a woman's dirtied purse, a fertilizer bucket, a rotting belt, a
laundry soap box, a bicycle upturned and without wheels.

Or by the game we play when we walk the graves—
Find the Craziest Name. *Wellborn. Lightfoot. Boney. Askew.*
And *Lucky*. We are alive.

Sarah Cortez

Locust

Swollen and hunched
into fetal crouch,

the small beast
has quit his split

shell. I find it
on a sidewalk

leading to nothing
of moment for me

today

except my present
memory clear

from childhood
when we hoarded

these translucent husks
thinking them too ugly,

yet too marvelous,
to squander.

Kay L. Cox

In the Land of the Urban Cowboy

Row after row of pickup trucks
cover the asphalt lot,
some with gun racks, bumper stickers
declaring their owners' love
for Darleen, Jimmie Sue or Verdanell.
It's Friday night at Gilley's,
payday.

Through wide doors past the ID check
a warm-up band is playing for couples
two-stepping round and round and round again,
her left hand hooked to his belt loop;
his right hand locked onto her shoulder.
Boots sweep the floor with soft swishy sounds,
fiddlers crank it up for the Cotton-Eyed Joe,
lines form on the dance floor.
The regulars are here,
wandering in from nearby plants,
the smell of the paper mill lingers on their clothes.
Reaching for a cold one and a cue stick,
they'll play a game or two or three
before heading home
to the waiting wife and kids,
paycheck partly gone.

Stan Crawford

Blues for Lightnin'

March. Late winter storm,
stinging rain, potholes on muddy side roads,

small, abandoned dogs slink slow, bitter,
growling at circling traffic. Air brake sighs,

battered trucks, a slammed tail gate. The hit
from the sound travels far in the gray air.

Rain now falling harder, faster, but
no Lightnin', no Lightnin' any more for

cold whiskey raindrops pint at a time,
fast-life women wearing red dresses, old friends

gone down on the turnin' row, guitar arpeggios
like bee swarms, honey and fire…

The blind fuse burns and burns. No more
cane on the Brazos. Sky smooth as a tombstone.

No more Lightnin' in the Third Ward. No more
Lightnin' to roll the bones. Gone, gone away, gone.

Carolyn Dahl

Christmas in a Snowless City

Plywood snowmen, outlined in red,
shimmy in the wind, spook
the dogs on their nightly walks.
Sprouting hedges tinkle with plastic
icicles and electric candles flame
in my windows, but never burn curtains.

A spiky door garland, creamed with fiber
snow and sprayed with pine scent, welcomes
a disheveled man who offers to paint
my address on the curb. "So your relations
won't get lost." He pauses, sniffs the air.
"Reminds me of cuttin' spruce with my Pa.
Snow thigh-high. Those trees cried all
the way home on the sled. I'd pick sap tears
from the snow. Chew 'em like bitter gum."

I give him the $25 because his mention
of snow makes him a type of relative
from my Christmas-card past. With
the whiskey breath of a favorite uncle,
he whispers, "I can't git the spirit here.
Not without snow." I slip him another ten,
am ready to invite him inside for chocolate,
a stray gift, a discussion of the virtues
of snow, but he pulls out his stencils
and spray cans and shuffles down the drive
to glitter the curb for relatives who won't
be coming. The paint can hisses. His face
flares briefly in the glow-in-the-dark color.
"Who can believe in snow angels
made of green grass.....anyhow."

Robin Davidson

Between Roses and Shadows: An Invocation

A found villanelle after Cy Twombly and Ingeborg Bachmann

What's true, above your grave, will tip the stone.
Night's cerulean spills shadows roses shadows.
What's true can part the earth just like a comb.

Wherever we turn in the storm of roses,
the night is lit up by thorns, and the thunder of leaves.
What's true above your grave, will tip the stone.

Oh how it grows dark. A handful of pain vanishes
and offers you the bowl of the heart.
What's true can part the earth just like a comb.

Shadows roses shadows. This cloud around me which I keep
as a house, *blue eye, blue* exile to lift the dead man up.
What's true above your grave, will tip the stone.

Great Bear, shaggy night, come down.
Cloud-furred one with old eyes, starry eyes, glimmering.
What's true can part the earth just like a comb.

Wherever the fire of roses is extinguished, an aria of
rain washes us into the river. O *blue rose of* night!
What's true above your grave, will tip the stone.
What's true does not buy time, it cancels it.

Note: Composed for the Menil Collection reading, "A Scattering of Blossoms," in response to Cy Twombly's 2008 painting of blue roses in "Untitled (Roses) Gaeta" which incorporates lines from Austrian poet Ingeborg Bachmann's "In the Storm of Roses." Of the 183 words comprising the title and body of this poem, only the nine italicized words pertaining to the color blue are mine. The rest are taken from Bachmann's collected poems entitled *Songs in Flight* and translated from the German by Peter Filkins.

Margo Davis

Music of the Spheres

After one of Da Camera's Inventors and Explorers concerts

I gaze into a telescope
that coaxes me toward Galileo's universe
as my weight leaves its grave position,
head and heart and balance flying and flaking like shooting stars
that seem to fall *up* and *away*,
never across, never
down to earth. I must rise with them,
little fragments of the self, bereft,
lightening the tenor of a cello lowing,
let go.
What harm, then,
in shedding flecks oxidized in dread,
each blue haze clearing the narrow portal
I must pass through, this make-shift hatch.

Diane DeGaetani

October 6th

It finally happened.
I finally looked at the Houston sun
right at midday and
my eyes were not burned
in their sockets.
It was one of the first cool days
after a long, drawn-out summer.
Even without water,
I did not feel parched at all.
There was a natural spring
of energy within me
and I was propelled.
It finally happened.
I put on a purple shawl
and I walked, walked, walked
and did not feel faint.

Winston Derden

Pothole Slalom

Pothole slalom, pothole slalom
missed one
missed one
missed one
got one.

One lane, two lane slalom,
      left/right, right/left
white lane-line,
your side   my side
mine, mine, mine.

Cratered slab
road rehab
asphalt scab
manhole cover
whip-the-wheel maneuver.

Dodge'm
hit'em
dodge'm   dodge'm,
      slalom,
home.

Carolyn Tourney Florek

Palmetto

I think it was a palmetto
    fanning green from a crack in the sidewalk
        along a busy boulevard

That convinced me I was living in a world
    where accidents happen in a tunnel of live oaks,
        their limbs a dark architecture shading

The ceaseless stream of traffic, a world
    of cross-fertilization between
        downtown and the outer limits;

Ideas and deals like pollen
    abundant in the air, for it's a competition,
        concrete against green,

Roads like rampant vines circling the city.

Turn our backs and the plants
    might just take over; concrete
        splitting for a single seed,

City springing ever further into green.

Dede Fox

Crossroads: Houston Street at Washington Avenue

Almost a century old,
the sturdy brick building
still smells improbably clean,
even with barred doors open
to welcome spring.

Only the scent of leather
from belts, batons, Bates boots
wafts through the rooms
of Central Police Supply, but
the structure, like Sixth Ward,
contains secrets.

Tucked away near the managers'
offices, wooden stairs creak, climb
to a balcony where girls and women
once bounced babies on covered knees
while below boys and men faced East
towards Jerusalem, opened sacred scrolls
adorned in velvet, silk, silver,
read hand-lettered words,
meticulous script on parchment
from the skin of a kosher animal.

In time acoustic tiles replaced
intricate pressed-tin ceilings,
a furnace the holy ark.
The women's gallery now extends,
into a second floor warehouse.

Outside the sandblasted façade reveals
blurred Stars of David, but
the Ten Commandments have drifted
as dust onto uneven sidewalks,
floated through gaping basement windows,
to coat horseshoes left behind in the old stable
once used by members of the synagogue.

As azaleas bloomed on Easter night in 1924,
a driver veered from Washington Ave.,
hit a bearded Jewish elder, who after prayers
walked towards his white frame house
with a latticework porch on Lubbock.

No one claimed the reward his family offered,
but newspapers noted his tragic death
with front page stories; a KKK ad on interior
pages invited citizens to a meeting where
"a spade is called a spade."

Priscilla Frake

Miss Houston Declares Her Favorite Month Is June

Favorite style: Rococo
Favorite clothing: Tropical-print hibiscus with drip-dry leaves
Favorite color: Wilted green
Favorite weather: Sticky, thick as tar
Favorite album: "Hotter than Hell" by Kiss
Favorite band: Cicada
Favorite slang expression: Packing heat

Adamarie Fuller

The Other Side of Paradise

I died on a day I've lived a thousand times, driving through concrete
    canyons.
Later I was vaporized, oxidized and boxed by a lazy clerk who switched my
    label,
sending a young boy to spend eternity with dusty Presbyterians,
and me to be gently planted in Miss Ima's gardens next to the dog Gilly.

As summer is sung to sleep by cicadas, we sit on the veranda,
    or chase fireflies
        along the lazy bayou.
Chilly evenings we lounge indoors on silk sofas, or watch winter visitors
admire decorated Christmas trees, remembering holidays they never had.
Azaleas weep fuchsia tears each spring for the gardener who no longer
    visits us.

Jeannie Gambill

Screech Owl

There is no screech. A whimsical neigh you pour
across our yard, our house. Your whickering trill
lures through wall and window. How spills
into this dusk-dusted interior
such gentle quaver? Perhaps your names store
some reason: Ghost Owl, Dusk Owl, Spirit,
Little Dukelet, Whickering, Shivering Owl.
And lore that escorts you from long before
might sign what you now are. Wisdom,
prophecy, aid, or—darker—you mean death
and mishap, imminent ill-will. I say
your genus fashioned of dream before breath
could dream its sound . . . here to unloose the day
to night, and me to your flickering call.

Elisa A. Garza

September 2008

My Hurricane Ike story
begins at the breast,
ends at the breast.
The middle is milky too.
My newborn, two weeks old,
nurses for hours, hardly resting.
This is the storm called baby;
she thinks only of herself.
She knows only the storm of hunger,
the rhythm of suckling,
a strong surge followed by calmer waves.
Because she is always at my breast,
we do not evacuate.
I am milking time, timing the milk;
time converts to milk.

My baby and I are communing,
we are nature, thinking only feed to feed.
I am too busy with now, with giving milk
to stockpile food or check our supplies.
My husband assures me we have enough.
Between nursings, I make more ice.

After night falls, I listen to the wind
while my baby sucks, her eyes wide open.
All night, she does not sleep, but does not cry.
Ike's winds howl and roar
their heavy metal lullaby:
my four year old sleeps, my baby eats.
My husband pushes the sofa
against our French doors
that bow slightly inside,
a push and pull dance
all night to Ike's guitar riffs.

By morning, Ike's music has played out.
The baby is tired and hot.
I fan her with cardboard,
drying off the sweat of our close feedings.
The radio announces how to help others,
where to go for ice, food, and shelter.
Knowing we are better off
than most, we pray our thanks
that the tree from our front yard
now lies in the driveway.
Then, the baby wants to nurse again.

John Gorman

Up from the Ruck

First you need desolation
the desolation, say, of an abandoned warehousing yard.
Trucks and rain, heat, the occasional freeze
that weakens macadam to cracking.
Piss, wind-blown dust, tobacco flecks
from discarded tins of Copenhagen.
Pollen, semen, spill of Mad Dog or Colt .45
all this forms a culture. A sandwich wrapper
becomes a tent to gather dampnesses
until some tree that can fend for itself
a cottonwood, say, or a camphor
arrives as a seed, sprouts, becomes a nonce
(if that's not too fancy a word) bonsai
then a wand, a stalk. No one pulls it up
because no one who comes down here—
dealers, users, cops, drunks, loners hoping
for a few hours of unmolested unconsciousness
—needs it. It's crass for poems to have morals
but this one says: When Nature Conspires with Wreckage
Over Just Enough Time, All Becomes Art.
The cottonwood by the shattered loading dock
might be by Courbet. Next somebody sensitive
but greedy too (this is Houston) sees the brutalized
brick of the warehouses, the wedge of crumbled gravel
as a piazza, cobbled, bedecked with Parisian
café tables, eco-responsible Italian fairy lights
Centrumspace (not over-restored) of The Cottonwood
a residential schematic for upwardly mobile young
urbanites. Meanwhile, out beyond the Beltway
a cloud of milkweed fluff hovers
where the rusted dumpster used to be
behind a decommissioned Taco Bell.

Maryann Gremillion

Glenwood

On Washington Avenue, gates open
a cemetery where tombstones speak,
an angel kneels, head on arm
the everlasting weep scrapes the edges
of sorrow for Lauretta Lucy Valentino,
only daughter of John and Lillian, died
May 27, 1878, aged 2 yrs, 3 mos, & 27 ds.
Ere sin could harm or sorrow fade. Death came
with friendly care. The opening bud to Heaven
conveyed. And bade it blossom there. Until
the day breaketh and the shadows flee away.
Tangled rosemary wild, azaleas weary.
Sunlight pokes the forgotten begonia.
Machines buzz near the bayou, spread
soft concrete for dogs people bicycles,
making room in the city, but not here.
A quiet hymn borne on fragrant air.

William Guest

Deliver This Letter

    to Augustus Chapman Allen
    and His Brother, John Kirby Allen

Dear Augustus and John:

Sorry I did not write to you sooner. But better late
than never, as they say. Letters usually travel geographically
but this one is aimed through time. I'm in Houston but don't know
where you're residing now. I hope our post office will fly
this letter to you.

When I first heard that you bought a big tract of land
in that new republic called Texas, near Harrisburg,
pretty far inland from the Gulf, along the banks
of a bayou stream, I wondered, have you lost your mind?
I was pretty sure you had.

Even though the price was low, it was swampy. Mosquitoes,
yellow fever, rain, heat? And you intended to subdivide
and find buyers? You bought in August 1836
and by January there were only twelve residents, one log cabin.
And a little ship named *Laura* made it to your site.

Your infatuation with that man, Sam Houston, I sort of understood.
The battle he won at nearby San Jacinto in just eighteen minutes
was amazing, taking from Mexico a huge piece of that country,
to start another country from scratch. But he had a questionable
Tennessee background you may have heard about. Used to live
with the Indians. Oh, well, he's probably not all bad but
I wondered if he was okay with having his name
tagged to your real estate scheme?

Well, those are thoughts I had at that time, but I began to see
people coming to Houston. Land sakes, I thought (pardon the pun),
what are they thinking? Who are they? Drunkenness, dueling,
brawling, prostitution and profanity, a wild mix of ego-mad types,
some were ladies and gentlemen walking in mud, mule-driven
street cars, a lot of slaves and left-over Indians. Conniving merchants,
deals in cotton, lumber, cattle. Later on: rice, oil, chemicals. Anything
for a buck. But oh that oil, that black liquid gold, bursting forth
millionaires like mushrooms from farms and ranchlands,
blue collars in the Shamrock Ballroom.

And more. Railroads crossing, mingling lanes that point
to anywhere, everywhere. I wondered how ships could ply
a drainage ditch (Buffalo Bayou it's called). But they did,
the way it's always done in Houston: dredge it, again
and again,
and make it what you want.

So naturally I began to watch. I heard a dreamy creed recited:
land, water and sky, and people will come. I looked and never
have I seen a sky so big, a night so bright, land so endless, and water
finding many places to surprise and flow.

I figured you would want to know what happened to your scheme
in that most unlikely spot. Well, Texas grew its legends and myths
of cowboys, guns, longhorns—and it's true, as one of the songs
of Texas says, the stars at night are big and bright.

Well, they came: Germans, Czechs, Irish, from all over the world
they came, making Texas, and your little town, into something mythical.
Though wrested from Mexico, its people are finding their land again.
A frontier, new, free, just bring your ambitions. And most of them arrived
through Houston, where many stopped, and stayed, dreamed and built.
Gleaming skyscrapers that even to you and your big-eyed friends
could exist only by imagination.

Look at Houston now! The fourth largest city in America, international,
proud, loud, gleaming and growing. From a swamp. Your swamp.

I hope you are well, wherever you may be. We are well, perhaps
as well as we think we are. You are entitled to a very big smile.

I eagerly await your reply.

       Your friend in Houston
       Bill

Laura Quinn Guidry

Sign of Contradiction

> *Francis of Assisi walked at right angles*
> *to all that characterized his age.*
> *He was a sign of contradiction.*
>   Mother Francis, PCC, Abbess
>   *The Cloistered Poor Clare Nuns*

The dog and I meander about campus on our early walk.
My morning ponderings as rambling as our path.
An insistent thought at the periphery.

A Franciscan sister walks the second story breezeway
between university buildings,
her head bent over the papers she is reading.

She is a silhouette, tall and purposeful, framed
for an instant by the black pillars and railing,
the symmetry of lampposts lined up

along the sidewalk below, and in the distance,
the street, parked cars, tunnel of trees.
I wonder what she is reading.

Morning is heavy and still.
Light from the lamps a contained glow.
The dog and I wander onto the grounds

of the Rothko chapel in the quiet neighborhood.
Houses on both sides of The Menil painted
grey and white like the museum.

I might like to live in one of those houses.
At my age, I'm immobilized by choices:
the gravity of *for the rest of my life*.

On the way back, our path meets the sister's.
At ground level, she is no taller than I am.
Below her brown habit, dirty white walking shoes.

She turns onto the quadrangle and continues—
a rhythmic following in footsteps—
while I, envy-ridden, head home.

Marian Haddad

Shakespeare for my Father

For Lynn Redgrave
Hamlet in Houston, Jones Hall

The stage-sized-large-as-living Michael Redgrave, facing us,
black and white sketch of him as Hamlet, the prince, behind her—
Truly, I was somewhat disappointed when—I'd found out there were not

more actors, not more pomp, in this show my dear brother took me to; I wanted
flash and fandango—but, I entered there, this one-woman playing many roles, ingenious
script—unfolding, how often had *To be or not to be*

filtered into—our ears, our eyes, as Hamlet
wondered if life should—go on—
the drudge and moan of it,

the clopping unfairness
of a life—ah, but
something like The Lord's

Prayer, or—The Pledge of Allegiance, the rote
recitation of words we did not stop long enough
to ever really hear—that night, became real, became

clear, as Lynn, mid-show, or nearer-closing, turned her back
to us, faced—her father, Hamlet—begged his wisdoms. And I heard,
as if, for the first time, real, alive—*Father, I want to be—an actor!*

Father! And she prodded him, almost god-like, for answers, quiet image
    bearing
more weight than a body, wanting him to give and be given—to answer;
    to be—or not to be
—*Father?* And the same small, but wide, words welled up inside me,
    outside me, the breath

in my body heaved and rose, for the beauty of understanding—
for the very first time, a meaning I might make clear, hear. *TO BE*
—*OR NOT TO BE—FATHER?* An actor. An any-

thing. *That,* my blessed master, is—
the question. I almost did not hear
the remaining words; caught up,

still, in the newness
of the old words,
the way poetry, itself, makes

something new—Lynn bowed, was done,
we rose with the power of our bodies, with the open-
ness of lungs, wanting to find ways to clap louder, to rise

up—to levitate, and we did, somehow, into the wide and high rafters;
my brother, fast-stuck two fingers, wide, into his mouth, whistled like a
    train searing
the night, the masses, thunderous in their applause, the baritone voices
    echoing, *BRAVO*

              and BRAVA!!!!! That night, the city, forever—
                      sent me—
                            singing.

Jerry Hamby

Arabella

The first spider in space
weaves like a drunken Jackson
Pollock, her web a tangle
of abstraction.

Encased in glass, she pulls thread
from spinnerets, lays it down
edge of frame until she finds
her bearings.

Free from earth's spin, she spins
in free form, drops a plumb
without aid of gravitational bob,
imagines a new geometry.

Draglines fly, angles and polygons
skew, polyhedrons blunt the panes
of her prison; she turns the spiral
orb in three dimensions.

Misunderstood and starving
artist, she will flame and flicker,
perish before her craft
slams to sea.

Michelle Hartman

Capricious Winds

        up to two hundred miles
an hour erased a line of town
as though it were a fourth grader's errant mark.
Scrubbed concrete slabs
between lumber skeletons
fringed by lace cuffs of torn houses.
News camera buzzards
gleaning information, comb the ruins.
Here, a wheelchair crushed
under front wheels of ruined vehicle
there a sodden teddy bear slumps
against shredded tree.
Then focus on single home, top floor gone,
outer walls in next town. The single wall
standing, covered in crosses.
A two-foot wooden cross,
painted lavender with raised
metal filigree fleur-de-lis;
surrounded, ceiling to floor,
wall to wall, with—
Celtic, Franciscan,
      Latin, Methodist
           St. Andrew, St. Bridget, Widow's Mite.

Each pristine as the day it was hung
by woman whose body
    was recovered in a tree
        one street over.

Bradley Earle Hoge

Emergence

I wake in time to see
a few stars
in the Houston morning
sky, the brightest,
reaching through
pollution of light,
ephemeral and eternal
at the same time
It reminds me that the Milky Way
is there, just like I've seen
it in the mountains,
and the desert
A road of stars spread across
the sky like a strand
of broken shells
along the beach
And if I close my eyes
these stars emerge
Because this is how
emergence happens
This is how God is found in flowers
deep in the woods,
how acts of kindness
become love, wafers and wine
become body and blood,
footsteps become the eightfold path,
traipsing over fossil
realities embedded in stone

Touch, sight, sound
embedded in flesh
Substance embedded
in the darkness
between the source
and the observance

Adam Holt

Poets Make Potholes Beautiful

Some mad energy gathered around today
Oh Houston
As I glided above Allen Parkway
After banging every pothole on Shepherd
Finally I knew how to say what to say.

If you knew me like I know you
Oh Houston and I hope you will
You would send me back to Dallas
In a heartbeat.

The fury within your son
Burns like anything people bring you—
Oil and meth and skin (they do)—
And you bring simmer to a boil (you do)
The slicks of oil on the coast
Oh Houston
Glug your name. I do the same.

Fourth largest city, beast slouching
Toward a refinery with slick lips
Not giving a damn for efficiency
Only the bottom line
Not a damn for rhyme for any reason
Not a damn for any season
But all the damns in all the lands for a dime
(Selah)

This is where I entice you
Oh Houston
A boy when I left now a man returned
Someone like the son of man spurned
By higher passions than a dime can earn
By Hermann Park and a painting in the Museum of Fine Arts
(It was a start)
That made me say when, lord, is enough?

When do the refineries refine themselves?
When does the bottom line bottom out?
When does a bayou become a boardwalk become an icon?
When does Space City look to the skies again and see more than rain?
There's a space station up there
Calling your name
Oh Houston
There's a country singer who does the same
Oh Houston
There's a rapper that does the same
Oh Houston
There's an oil baron with his hands upon your ears
Oh Houston
They all want something different
And I just want you.

If you will rise and burn
For something other than sex and wealth
If you will consider your health—
You're at that age where it pays to take care of yourself—
To talk to your doctor about fill in the _____
To talk, to talk, to listen to your sons and daughters,
To me,
Oh Houston.
Even minor poets can shape you.
You need us—
Poets brave enough to rhyme their rhymes in public places
And demand public art and light rail in all the wrong places.

You know us. The ones best sent
To the first and second coasts
Or banished to Dallas,
Or confined to coffee shops in Montrose
Or Valhalla on Rice campus.
Poets make potholes beautiful.
Poets like the one you here read
Oh Houston,
Space City, Clutch City, my city, in need.
Indeed.

Cindy Huyser

No Accident

It was hot that day, June,
the air thick and humid.
I saw red and blue lights
later, found the bloated body
in the pages of the newspaper
next day, the outline of my walk
clawed into a plan—as if
someone else had chosen
when I would leave
or the way I would go,
my own luck floating
on the water, around me
like an angel or a shielding cloud.

Angélique Jamail

The Complicated and the Simple

Oh Mexico, glorious land of contradictions, a mystery
my childhood observations couldn't reconcile,
the Blessed Virgin, sexless mother of a benevolent
dual-natured god, was less inscrutable than you.

You, the assumed homeland of every brown-skinned immigrant
who worked with his hands for a living, who kept his eyes
down in the presence of the natives, the homeland of every
Spanish-sounding name that found its way onto the local news.

But then my parents enjoyed your pristine beaches, your resorts
where every guest room had its own private swimming
pool, hibiscus blooms floating lazily across the water,
your charming villages where their dollars-turned-pesos

enabled so much for so little. Then they came home:
suitcases brimming gifts like embroidered cotton
blouses and gold earrings and stiff burro dolls with yarn hair;
cameras glutted with pictures of sunsets and the ocean and

floral centerpieces and food; and my mother wearing some
new colorful, sweeping skirt that skimmed her ankles. Oh
precious sun-kissed coast of tanned and perfumed tourists,
you were the land they escaped to once a year, refugees

from their work and children for five days every October.
Mexico, land of love and leisure, land of rest, how different
you must have been from the dusty leavings your
people brought with them to Houston, those struggling

immigrants whose children played in the parking lot of
the sagging wooden apartments across the street from our home;
the strangers my mother would caution us against
bringing home to play with in our large backyard cool

with trees, our swimming pool, our house that was
big enough; the pranksters who stole our bicycles and Christmas
lawn ornaments, who shot pistols at the moon every Cinco
de Mayo. Oh Mexico, we ate your dinner and wore your finery,

we beat your piñatas at every celebration. In school we sang
your folk songs and pretended to learn your language. We
put tropical flowers in our hair and gobbled down my
mother's homemade margarita cheesecake.

But we never embraced you, we never let you touch us.
We never stretched past the border of the front yard. Forgive
us our distance, our walls, our fences, our disdain. Forgive
us for taking what we wanted and leaving the rest.

Joshua C. Jones

Spring in Houston

After Sean Hill

Spring hum-mumbles its favorite blues tune
of the first riding mowers and spits the bitter
click of fantailed sprinklers rapping on the back
windows. Our Dallas friends say it's too soon
for daffodils, assume another frost will wither

them to the ground. Late February afternoon,
forced into shorts, we watch starlings skitter
over fries and onion rings spilled out of a Jack-in-
the-Box bag. Now, daylight vies with the moon
to reclaim six p.m., but I'll miss the early dark,

the halo reeking off 59, the grackle immune
to shame or cold pecking the grass, critters
silent underground for three months. Hewn
from bayou, the city will smell like food truck fritter
and saltgrass. The impenetrable Houston black

clay will soften and make yard work opportune;
so I'll give in to a request more like an order
from a friend I owe, leaving my own yard strewn
with last year's debris, an unopened letter.

Claire Kageyama-Ramakrishnan

The Backyard Garden in Houston

Grass seeds and shifting salamanders wake the creatures below.
Beetles trundle through the top layer of fertile soil.

Crisp divots of transplanting absorb air and light.
Dispersal of ladybugs inhibits the spread of aphids.

How clever the chameleon is to camouflage itself as clover.
And the gopher, idiosyncratic as ever, lapses from furrowing.

Irritated by the musty commotion, it gnaws the inveterate pipes.
The soaker hose responds with trickles, then a surge of warm water.

It's the chlorinated kind that strips hair of its natural shade.
In this city, hard water bleaches every head with locks.

My hair, once black, turns red, dulls from rust to brown.
In mirrors under halogen, I see haphazard strands of orange.

Chlorinating kills the germinating suspects.
Fluoridating keeps the tooth enamel from wearing.

A fledgling lands on the lip of a brimming seed jar.
The seeds spill, frightening the fledgling into awkward flight.

The wind tosses blue buttons, phlox, and sunflower seeds.
The ground needs something besides Harlequin beetles.

In the end everything thrives to wither and reseed itself.
Scientists say creatures will plant, continue to thrive.

The raven eyeing carrion drops a half-eaten apricot.
A weathered hand assists a smooth, gloved hand.

The neighbor's owl hoots as creatures dig and scrape.
The blue jay snickers as fingers plant dahlia and tulip bulbs.

Sterilized steel clippers land on a heap of peat moss.
They join the company of cotton swabs and alcohol.

Laurence V. Kelly

Houston Vignettes

West Montgomery Road
Brown-eyed, beautiful Gypsy girls.
Third Ward girls, their net worth
In a chain of gold pieces around their ankle.
Lightnin' Hopkins at a Juke Joint way out Westheimer.
Even pheasants out west of town.
Freed blacks in Third Ward
Before the Allen Brothers.
Four Palms Club on Telephone Road.
Buffalo Bayou flyway. Cranes, plovers, pelicans
In River Oaks back yards.
West University sweeping for Spanish gold in
What remains of the Old Spanish Trail.
Prison Farm ghosts still haunting in Mission Bend.

Jim LaVilla-Havelin

J.R.

I have seen one of the great arms of my generation
homeless under a bridge in Houston
lost to fame, teammates, dark dome, self

and if the oranges, yellows, golds—bands across
an infamously bad uniform design
were meant somehow to convey Texas sunlight

J. Rodney Richard's home beneath the bridge in darkness
hollowed out the lie—an imposing figure on the mound,
a ferocious competitor—to see him come to this

and then salvation, was a lesson in humility and loss,
in racism and cost, in natural gifts and shocks
beyond the stats behind the baseball card, the lives.

Catherine Lee

Bird Watching on the Roof

Stars penetrate the chalky black
like weeds cracking through asphalt.
I only come here at night—
when the rooftop gardens stretch
into meadows in my periphery,
and intimates flapping on lines
in the daytime scorch are now
tendrils of lilies in the breeze.
Even impatient sirens fade
to nothing in this place.

The pine warbler, yellow and small,
peeks from her nest.

I am like her.

We call to others of our kind.
We pick at twigs and little things
until our home is made, cleaving
to eaves built by other hands.
There are colorful scraps of plastic
woven in with the natural fibers.
Stronger.

She watches me.

Thad Logan

Hello From . . .

Houston, 1957. Space City
it will soon be called; Sputnik
circles in the night sky.
We still could see the night sky
from our backyard in town.

Everything looked new, that year,
the year they moved the old school
way out in the tangly woods,
where they'd scraped the sandy earth
bare, and planted low, colorful classrooms,
and concrete playground pads.

Out there coach taught us
to blow our noses, in second grade;
inside Señora Carroll sweetly trilled
"El perro esta corriendo" and
Larry threw up in the eraser tray.

Looking out big wide windows
waiting for the time to pass
I made a hospital for broken pencils.
Steve drew minute, intricate airplanes,
in fantastic flight careening
around and off the page, and tiny men
with big round heads, fragile sticks
in spacesuits.

At recess we wandered, restless,
digging holes sometimes to see
how big they could get. How far
we could go.

But mostly I went to the far corner
by myself, back where the pines still stood,
where there were birds, sometimes. And flowers
like little purple hands, waving to me
from some other country
where I belonged.

Janet Lowery

Wild West

Not many poets show up to two-step
at country western clubs sprinkled like diamonds
along main drags and back streets in Houston,
but each night the poetry of spent hearts
and renewed romance circles the crowded floor
in triple time along the line of dance.

Heart-shaped rhinestones pasted across
the back pockets of girls' jeans sparkle like crystals;
at wrists the click of glass and gold,
at necklines a circlet of silver and stones,
moonlight crusted across eyelids and earlobes—
it's like opening night at the Houston Grand Opera.

Men's ornate belt buckles accent western shirts
tucked into pressed and creased denim,
finished off with cowboy hats and boots—
except, that is, for veteran dancers. Dressed
in un-tucked button-downs, old denim,
and sneakers re-soled for slip and slide,
they're the pros that weave partners
through the crush of couples under disco balls,
faux starlight, and the mirror-studded saddles
suspended like seraphs from ceiling beams.

Wistful rhymes about Bibles and beer,
radios and rodeos, small towns, old dogs,
and dusty roads lace plaintive refrains yearning
for a world so many miles back, so many
lifetimes ago, but it's the ride of a blue slide
on a pedal-steel guitar, the plucked strings
of mandolins, banjos, and country violins
that quicken the feet yet stay the soul, like
jewel-tones struck by the hand of Orpheus.

Anne Robinson Mabry

Nothing to Report

Nothing to report
Except the in and the out
The constant hum
The show in motion
The shift of light

Nothing to report
Except the pumping of blood
The sensations of flesh
The light and color
The warmth of sun

Nothing to report
Except the sound of traffic
The footfalls and trains
The remote conversation
Laughter and glasses and ice

Nothing to report
Except the hummingbird
Paused just now for nectar
And is gone.

Dodie Messer Meeks

Green

If you are up high enough
Tower
High rise
Campanile
Plane gliding in
If you look out and down
Houston is green.

All of it cushiony
Mansions and shrubbery
Sculptures and sprinklers
Houston is green.

Somewhere down under there
Are boarded up windows
Bodies in bayous
Bail bondsmen
Guns for sale
Jobless guys drinking.

But, my friend, most of it,
I want to say all of it,
Fate, chance, kings,
Desperate men,
If you can get up high enough
It spreads out
A tapestry
Eight shades of green.

John Milkereit

Houston

Tonight, driving along Richmond Avenue
trying to remember a favorite poem,
reciting a few lines,

I pass a ballroom and toss words
that land against a window or only the door.
I open the moon roof and say the darkest lines.

I stop at a red light near the Texaco and begin another stanza,
then stumble after passing the venue of the last poetry book signing—
an art gallery filled with an obbligato of oil paintings

that copy someone else's oil paintings. There is a line about stars,
but I can't see any. I forget the rest of it, then promise
to read it later, then I recall the reading at Rice.

It's the one about a workshop that critiques
a poem about a drawbridge operator,
and possibly death, and somehow a mouse.

I can't help but see how enormously
tempting traps baited with cheese must have been
for a mouse that lived near a drawbridge operator.

I see in the windshield, the drawbridge
operator above with clouds that seem like
marshmallows. And I'm the mouse scurrying below.

When I look in the rear-view mirror, I'm the operator
with my fishing line nibbling—I like nibbling
better than jigging—and the mouse is brushing its teeth.

Afterwards, I see you, the operator
I love with zipped-up leather boots. I am the fish
hooked on your line, fighting you anyway,

but I feel like we're indoors in our bedroom somehow
with that faded wallpaper, and the mouse has left its home
and moves as fast as the bayou into our attic.

Terry Jude Miller

Lightning and Grackles

from my office window
I watch steel clouds
slowly overtake Williams Tower

an argument of grackles
bursts from beneath the hedge grove
by the parking garage
and reassembles in feeble protest
upon the freshly mown lawn

the sky clears its baritone throat

powder puff flashes behind
the darkening gray
soothsay the coming spectacle

a lightning bolt slices
across the phallic tower—
an "X" of nature
and man-made ornament

then a cannon clap
of thunder that sends
objecting grackles west
to chase sunlight and silence

Jane E. Mulholland

Audacious Lady

Neither fine Roman beauty, nor coy Parisian courtesan,
Airport escape exposes her backside.
Urban debris: billboards, strip centers,
Bread wrappers, whiskey bottles and Bud cans,
Furniture filled tent, "WE SAVE YOU MONEY!"
Greet the new arrival.
Horrified—our new home.
Tucked in a northern suburb
Four bedrooms, two and a half baths
Odd corporate couple my teenage son and I.
No zoning allowed;
Instead, Draconian subdivision rules.
All newcomers marvel,
"So much house—so little money."

Four-mile drive to park-and-ride
"We are making good time,"
The driver muses, "If we are moving."
The bus produces solace;
Company van pool brings torment.
Near downtown billboards vanish,
Roads a quagmire of cloverleaves.
Shimmering in the morning light
City rises like corn in an Iowa field.

Goofy her fun:
Art cars with their own parade;
Beer can house an aluminum curiosity.
Two guys with blessings from their wives,
Marry a tree on Menil lawn.
Tree planted in yard for all to enjoy.

Fun is ok, but no bigamy allowed,
The tree came down.
This lady beguiles and smiles
Always in many styles.

"Most diverse," Rice professor asserts.
Catholic friends grasp hands, bow heads,
Murmur prayer before dinner.
A Hindu friend folds her hands, shuts her eyes,
Praying as our lunch arrives.
Witness to adulthood at Bar Mitzvah;
Celebrate silken cords tied on waists of two Zoroastrian boys.
Our Culture Eating Club fancies Afghan best,
Delights in Thai, Ethiopian, Cuban, and Italian;
Learns difference between Indian and Pakistani.
Neighborhood restaurant Chinese vegetarian,
Where blushing waitress prefers husband,
Bows and invites us to Buddhist conversion rite.

In spring I wait.
Daily pass grassy hills
Above concrete walls to contain deluge.
The unfolding comes slowly.
First mallows white and dainty pink appear.
A fleck of blue announces, "Bluebonnets are coming!"
Orange Indian paintbrushes self-selected
Protect the field, foretell the riot to come.
Today is the time.
Green hill a backdrop for the stage
Covered in blue blooms
Dappled with orange, yellow, and magenta flowers,
Audacious lady claims her due.

Mark Stephen Mullee

Baytown

Although the sign says not to swim,
and not to eat the crabs that swim
in water the refineries have fouled,
still I hear the wild but muffled
shouts of boys entering the water.
Their young and able bodies dot the water
like buoyant marshmallows sweetening
the surface of a chemically contrived
chocolate-flavored drink. In the deepening
dusk I watch them swim ashore, alive
in spite of everything, towels underfoot
ready to receive their rash-red feet.

Carol Louise Munn

Severity

What we water in July may live
or may curl black onto one stalk
dark in the crisp ground.

So begins the middle
of a Houston summer:
birds fighting over the birdbath,
bats flitting above the empty lot
next door. Morning glories thin
on the vine, brown strings
tying the yellowed leaves
together. Only the oleander
thrives in drought.
Pink petals extend the length
of branched spires reaching
for sun. We wake early
for the respite before dawn
when we work outside
trimming visible death.

We fix iced tea to tide
us through the afternoon
when heat will rise like mountains,
certain as the will to survive.

Sheryl L. Nelms

Bologna Sandwiches

Gramps always
took me with him

to the Highway 45 Market in Houston

he'd have
the meat man
cut thick slices

from the fat
roll of bologna

then Gramps would
pick a fresh loaf
of white

Wonder Bread

and a jar
of horseradish mustard

we'd go home
and Gram

would fix a plate
full of sandwiches

we'd sit
on the screened-in north porch
and eat those sandwiches
drink sweet tea

and watch
yellow sulphur butterflies

hover over
the orange zinnias

in their Victory garden

Stella Nesanovich

Houston: December 2008

Water trails in roadside culverts
as we edge through traffic's snarl.

First dark, a view of broken trees—
no New England ochre autumn.

Here, remnants of Hurricane Ike,
the sun's circuit completed.

Still, time for pleasure:
a rich curry at Thai Spice,
a new film, the Menil.

Morning brings another feast:
Dim Sum with friends.

Beyond your window,
the stained glass from New Orleans,
a Shumard oak has shed its leaves.

Few cling to spidery branches,
gray bark of winter's chill.

David Olson

Copperhead

At home in piney woods—
this dogwood-scented Eden
where vines climb sassafras,
sweetgum and loblolly pines—
I trespass my backyard garden's
primeval wilderness with care.

Here, awaiting unwary prey,
in dry leaves or poison sumac
undergrowth, in camouflage
of rusted browns, might lurk
a lethal viper's beaded eye,
sensing tongue and tensing coils.

Trilla Pando

Montrose Monostiches

Arise. Find shoes, feed cat, fetch coffee—

Fluffy feral felines demand al fresco meal. Inside, heart softens.
No sun, gray day, rushing sirens shriek city music; radio plays classical.
Oak roots challenge roller-coaster sidewalk. Be careful walking.
Turmoil! Agitation! Dried-out leaves swirl across empty parking lot.
Broken Obelisk stands tranquil guard. Calmness reigns, then the poodle plunges.
Rothko darkness brings time, brings calm, brings light. Then out, into sun.
Pink rose discarded on brick sidewalk pleads to tell her story.
Bright, then dark, mostly sunny Menil Park: a palette of green swatches.
Shy sequestered poppy shows her glowing face to sun-drenched afternoon.
Clouds streaking across pink-stained tree-framed evening sky. An ode to joy.
Shining promise, library beckons through the dusk, "Come—book, chair, time."
Wet grass on bare feet, evening pleasure touches sole. Night's gentle frolic.
Dark street, lonely owl, neon windmill standing sentry. Montrose midnight—

fix coffee, feed cat, shed shoes. Chillax.

Mary Parham

Being a Poet in Houston

Eyelids drooping, drooling at the mouth,
sweat dripping from its brow and breathing
heavy, the August afternoon watches me.
You sprawl drowsy in the lawn chair.

I'm a poet: it's my job to wake you,
make you see like a child that blue
mosquito hawk on the cyclone fence,
make you smell the grass just mown.

I must metamorphose into the queen
ant fiercely pumping pheromones,
lead you with the faint perfume of words
through scarlet membranes and cell walls
into the cool grottoes of your cerebral cortex.

But now my pen's hot ink smells like crude oil,
not new-mown grass, and I see you've folded
my poem into a coaster for your longneck.
It's just too hard. I'm no queen ant,
and I'm dozing off in the 4 o'clock heat.

Richard H. Peake

Seeking Texas Sandhills

All of the gray-brown giants are gone
from meadows where flocks were feeding
only days before. Yesterday
we saw a family of three,
a brown young bird and its parents.

My wife sighs her disappointment
as she looks into empty fields.
This daily ride to flocks of cranes
gives her pleasure that's not forgot.
She senses kinship to these birds.

Late fall will bring migrant flocks back
to spend winter on these grasslands,
and we will ride the afternoons
glad to have weathered one more year
to greet them as they forage there.

Though our bodies show signs of wear,
days and months, a year of aging
has not diminished joy of life
or hope both of us can greet cranes
as they trumpet a safe return.

Donna E. Perkins

To Work

Slow-witted morning, dense
fog from too much life, not enough sleep.
Merging into morning's rush hour,
grateful I'm outbound traveling 70
for much of my 30 miles.
Traffic parts around timid
fools going the speed limit.
We're an angry river surging around rocks.
A billboard reminds that Jesus loves me,
a bail bond ad, a smear of dog, the rise
of bridge over the Houston Ship Channel.
Early sunlight crosses the industrious port.
I am of the hordes indentured to miles
of refinery lights and petroleumed air.

Elina Petrova

Soon

Give me the least inspiring subject
and I'll write a poem whose happiness
won't fail in complexity. Like now: rain
pours. Andrés Orozco-Estrada—high
on caffeine before conducting Dvořák's
7th in D minor—sleeks his wavy black hair
backstage at Stude Hall, changes the brown
Ralph Lauren shirt that doesn't match his pale
determined face. I wait outside, taking photos
from afar behind a stranger in black, resting
against the vertical aperture of James Turrell's
Twilight Epiphany—the grassy, truncated
pyramid's atrium under the illuminated
roof with clouds in its opening.
In my forties, I'm in a way sixteen—
the same sixteen when I thought I'd soon
meet someone who celebrates rain like I do,
that life should resist the adjective "lukewarm"—
the word Andrés teases his orchestra
on rainy, unenthusiastic Mondays.
Drenched, I lean against a student's bicycle
to snap pictures, anticipating Andrés's
conducting fiesta—his grasshopper's leap
in the tight Nehru jacket, and that impulse
akin to my naïve, explosive happiness—
duende of cherry blossoms under swollen
graphite sky that rains into this poem

where the stranger in the atrium stares
at the courtyard of Rice's School
of Political Science; the woodwind section
straightens music stands for cross-rhythms
of Dvořák's furiant dance, and my hands
adjusting the objective lens at *Epiphany*
are wet, but never lukewarm.

Dustin Pickering

Houston Has Lifted Me, Yet In Stillness

The moon is motionless over the same city
that harbors Johnson Space Center.
This is where miracles began in years
and where they are final.

Tonight the sharply defined thumbnail
of the soul sister of our sky
reminds us dreams are not cowards,
that even cowards can become brave.

I do not aspire to climb higher;
my wish is to merely be.
Earth is my fortress
and I hide my reluctance here.

Houston has lifted me, yet in stillness
I am a promise.
Roses open like memories of kind acts,
scoring the humble many points.

The doctor privately keeps record
of our teary-eyed Man in the Moon.
Like a silver piece of bone,
his smile invites us to sink deeper.

I allow the doctor to stitch up wounds
of my arrogance,
although the stillness of night hangs forever
like a thief in dreams.

henry 7. reneau, jr.

The Holiness Church of Houston, TX

their Bubba trucks &
plastic Jesus on the dash
their blind faith
                 as pervasive as dust
as religious as gridiron Sundays
luck as a residue
of intelligent design: Go, Texans!!
stumbling
about simultaneous vastness &
                           enclosure

& no good deed goes unpunished

their theory of everything
         like loose metal fragments
in a combustion
engine: breaks things &
causes leaks &
                vital gears seize—
the way a puddle ripples
      from the trespass of a pebble
 does not operate
             the way they want it to
                or think it should—
hoped it would—but always other
                    than it does
like erratic footfalls
in broken shoes of homeless
                desperation
       a collective consensus
     traveling bigger than light
from which their universe derives.

Lynn C. Reynolds

Buffalo Bayou

Dark as shadow
Green as spinach
 (mostly dirty brown)
You grew a village
Then a town
Then a metropolis.

The Allens advertised your banks.
Called it Houston.
You brought boats, food, fashions,
Hoards of mosquitoes
And muddy flood waters.

Then came
Skinny dippers,
Fishers,
Rock skippers,
Waders, peace seekers,
Bicyclers, Sunday picnics.
The Reeking Regatta.

You flooded one time too many and so
You were shoved, redirected,
Narrowed,
Concreted into new parts that never run over.
No one comes to you there.

When all is said and done
And the humans leave for space
You will keep running,
Brown and dirty,
Breathing life around a dying city.

Sally Ridgway

Streetlights Across the Bayou's Ribs

Fish leaping. My soundless automatic feet, ridges
in the grass, roaches seeking water. Looking west
to the pale end of day, I want to grab what
little's left. Already east's a tarnished sky, inky water,
an ibis silhouette. Trees wag brittle tongues.

Back home, beside the driveway, my dog's grave.
My palms on the pebbles want her pearly fur now
buried in a towel, chest crushed, eyes open. Dirt,
dog hairs make a web, wilted begonias, cross of twigs.

The hose trickles to the pool. Cicadas click.
All night, the earth is cracking. In bed, my body
sears the vast sheets. I roll from sheaths of wishes and
regrets till mourning doves' suede coos from the cypress.

Gary S. Rosin

Rush-Hour Fugue

Stuck in the usual

rush-hour traffic, impatience
clenches like a fist.

Somewhere out of sight,
another anonymous
nuisance or tragedy clogs every lane.

It doesn't matter that you're late.
It doesn't matter that your engine
is running hot. It doesn't matter that

you don't know why.

It doesn't matter. You are still
going nowhere. Just ahead,

a Cadillac convertible, its top down.
A bald, middle-aged man,
caught without a hat.

Low-rider low, the Cadillac
bounces and sways in place,
rocks as if winding along

the road not taken.

Varsha Saraiya-Shah

Seven Rishis of Allen Parkway

> *For J. Plensa's* Septuplet of Sculptures *on Allen Parkway,*
> *known as* Tolerance

Men of mesh-steel, seated
        on Spanish boulders.
They stand for seven continents.
Sit with them to be of their tribe.
No need to prove your creed or be of certain nation,
        speak Spanish or know English.
Round the clock on Harmony Walk
        they receive joggers, couples, amblers alike.

They hold open a myriad of books
with see-through letters,
symbols, and numbers in multiple tongues:
Hebrew, Hindi, Arabic, Greek, Korean.
No book is barred.

The colossal oaks of their alcove remind me
of the distant cousins,
Neem trees of my native land.

Beside them I bask in the dusk
draping the Buffalo Bayou in a sari—
saffron turning purple over the Rosemont Bridge
clouds unfurling feathers eastward

I hear sounds of *kirtan*, the steady beat
of temple bells, devotees singing
hymnals with cymbal, the *dhol*. Air infused
with sandalwood incense, lamps stars alight
on the Bayou at twilight—
A dawn will break soon on that land,
thousands of miles away.
Letters bring us together, I hear the Rishis murmur.

Note: *Rishi* is a Sanskrit word for a sage; *kirtan* means devotional group singing; *dhol* is a two-sided drum.

Jenna Pashley Smith

A Texas Initiation

A tunnel of earthen rubble mystifies
this Midwestern native and her
just-walking son,
whose curious steps soon become wails.
Ripping off pants and diapers, thwarting
crimson biters with frantic hands,
we are baptized in boils,
casualties received from the jaws of the
fire ant hordes.

Loueva Smith

Zoe Returns

When she came home
after thirteen years,
pregnant and alone,
having seen all the great
cities of Europe,

she told her brother
it was hideous.
Only in Houston are the birds obscene.
Grackles hoard twilight.
All the gold belongs to them.

Their racket is louder
than the traffic,
their throats equipped
with short wave radio static.
There are enough

of them to carry off a cat,
or a little dog, my pretty,
or a baby, or Zoe's lost heart.
She looks one in the eye.
It is yellow.

A lemon eye.
Black wings are satin
shook from a cinder box
and glittering blue
in the noonday sun.

Rebecca A. Spears

The Drive Home

Here, the last broad avenue,
last stretch home
                    after a funeral.
It's winter, and trees stripped bare
cluster so thickly I can hardly
see into the groves.

At this intersection of woodlands,
city and prairie, a javelina
on the grassy median
                    lies
defeated
      bristled brown, eyes closed,
destined for the city dump.

Did this happen last night?

I know the risks driving in blackness
this nature preserve circling
Armand Bayou,
                antlered buck and soft doe
a still life in my headlights.

Along the brackish bayou where life
begins and renews, I remember
cancer startling my friend, then
wrecking her will.
                Her final wish
to go on and on someplace
                    not earth.

Some evening on this road, I may catch
young javelina in the carlights, watch
them graze on the median
                             —safe
for an interval—
                    cars plowing by
on either side. It has happened before.

Now a turtle plunks into green water.
A linen web stretches between branches.
An egret flies up.
                A mile away my house,
my husband, my children wait
and I am late coming home.

Sandi Stromberg

Implosion

Sunday, 8 January 2012

We showed up at 5 a.m. to escort media
a safe distance across the street. A wall
of windows on the 24th floor inviting

city-wide views. But fog held everything
in its gray embrace. Houston. The Medical Center.
The condemned structure—once Prudential's

celebrated Taj Mahal. A symbol of beauty
as memorable as the Rock of Gibraltar,
the building passed her final day awaiting

execution. Her hidden guilt—the asbestos,
eroded limestone, weakened steel girders.
Old-timers reminisced. Their first swim

in the building's pool. Tennis matches on her courts.
Preservationists bemoaned the death of yet another
Houston landmark. While those who'd worked deep

inside her crinoline maze waited, feelings mixed.
Everyone held in this time out
of time. The way we wait through life's delays—

the births, a loved one's death, inevitable events,
large and small. And when we'd almost despaired,
clouds did part. And the building made her final

grand appearance center stage. Her fragile footprint
still intact. All eyes breathed a last, long look.
The sharp reports came. For a moment, nothing.

Then, like a proper Southern lady, she fell
elegantly. Legs tucked under her skirts.

Larry D. Thomas

The Mausoleum

Montrose Bar, Houston, TX

Outside, in what was once a front yard,
when the wind blows, a dead tree creaks,
laden with its fruit of white masks.

Inside, in the smoke-filled shadows,
works of art deliciously macabre
lurk in every nook and cranny.

During the open mike,
as the poets sweat,
wresting the sounds of their images

in the unforgiving glare of the spotlight,
the critics, tête-à-tête
on their lofty perches at the bar,

confer like cloaked lepers,
fueling their whispered diatribes
with swigs of cold stout.

Nancy Thorleifson

Em on the Red Line

Because Death would not stop for me
I hastened after her
The metro held the two of us
And many in between

The rocking hum along the rails
Gave time to frame my plea
With ease she pierced my yearning eyes
And waited patiently

Around me all the dying thrived
In hospitals, on streets
Between the glass and asphalt grey
Among the vibrant well

"O Mistress Pitch, do not withhold
The gift of healing dark
The respite of long night's recline
The respite of no dawn."

The train car stopped and emptied out
No station sign at hand
The ceiling lights were freshly dim
No colors, edges, sound

Eternity surrounds me now
No crispness of that time
I barely sense the thanks I felt
When first she lent her ear

Margo Stutts Toombs

Batwing

Chicks love the Batwing
Art car of cool steel
Birthed by the hero of the hood.
Sculpted with an art heart.
Torches blaze as he roars past my window.
Teeth grills grin from glass and dashboard
Skull eyes flame from side windows
Chicks see a cool dude in the driver's seat.
I see a hero.
Chicks love the Batwing.
I love the Bat.

Elizabeth Tornes

Visiting Houston

For Anne, Julie, and Molly

As I sat in the Rothko chapel
between the two older sisters
sitting in silence
I thought of you, Molly.
The darkness that engulfed you
as the purple-black paintings,
that heavily shadowed space,
engulfed us that day. The mystery
of your self-inflicted death
has congealed over time
and transits ("What is not transformed,
is transferred.") into our lives
twenty years later. They told me
about the lonely years you spent
living with your husband in Puebla,
Mexico, raising your daughter
who was only seven when you died.

The heaviness of the story,
nearly unbearable, only lifted
that evening, when I met
your daughter Liz.
She has your deep blue eyes,
your thin, arched eyebrows
(as if constantly surprised),
your easy laughter.
She is wily, funny,
and smart, just like you.

Your voice lives on
in her throaty Spanish
as she orders your favorite
poblano dish at a Mexican restaurant
our last night together in Houston.

It would be easy to say
you were there with us,
but you weren't. God knows
what happened to you, alone
that impenetrable night
in the hospital.

But Molly, coyote of the darkness,
whenever I think of you,
your daughter's laughter
breaks through like the morning sun.

William Turner

Yellow Oily Cloud

Those who walk below
Cannot see or know
The yellow oily cloud
Hanging like a shroud.
A yellow pus-filled sty
On the eyelid of the sky
Seen East, South and West
From a corporate tower best.

The cloud is slowly closing.
Silently it is flowing.
Across the land flossing.
While the millwork is spewing.

Gasoline and plastic
Wraps walkers in mastic.
Below like disappearing ink,
It's the misty yellow stink
That curls about the houses
Where walkers fall asleep.

Evangelina Vigil

emancipation park

by day the jointed aching limbs of ancient oaks
lean low in the directions of time
laden with the weight of knowing:
moss that clings
cryptic exchanges
the passing of the bottle in a wrinkled paper bag
coarse hand to coarse hand
gulps, grunts

by night the jointed aching limbs of ancient oaks
lean low in the directions of time
laden with secrets where darkness is light:
whisperings and sighs
the groping for the needle
the feel of the powder
the giving work of someone's mother
someone's daughter

now dawn, dew slithers down the rough bark
glistening sweat of the steamy summer night
while in the center of the park
deep in the shadows of ancient trees
a lone figure sits on a bench, motionless
he gazes blankly at moss-stained table of cement:
the crack of continents
the pieces of the puzzle

the jointed aching limbs of ancient oaks hold their pose
leaning low in the directions of time
shadows hovering, cradling:
rays of sunlight pierce the haze
a teardrop glistens
like dewdrops on sparse tufts of grass
like tiny bits of broken glass
amber, indigo and emerald green
on the sandy littered lot

Randall Watson

The Busy

A weed rises from my neighbor's gutter.
Sparrows gather to drink from the clog.
Just this morning, fog
made the windows hard to see through,
the pale, white micro-beads
fading in first heat.

Such is the nature of my coming and going.
Oh dear one, I say, oh brother, oh sister,
oh moving family, greeting the age.

Look at the lawn—topsoil thin on the almost clay.
The husks and soon-white seeds
of the Chinese tallow,
the rippled bark of its bad wood
filled with tiny shadows.

What is it that a word can measure
where every metaphor is filled with distances?

What does it join to itself, that wet possum
burrowing its way into the spaces in the walls
to make its sleep?

Weasel

Hunger

i see him digging through the trash as
i fill up my car; rose stems for fingers
digging for the little crumbs we take
for granted. his eyes are filled with a
weariness only the desperate would
understand, the hunger fueling his
frenzied search amidst the cold air.

i've seen him before, every morning
under the freeway, sleeping through I-45
traffic and construction. the workers
ignore him, knowing there is no
other place to welcome him.

this man digs through torn credit card receipts
and spoiled yoohoo cartons, only to find
hunger deep within the bottom of the bag.
body quivering, he turns to wander off.
sleep should come to him soon, but what
comfort is there in slumber when the
frozen air attacks you? i shake the final
droplets of gasoline into the tank and
grab my uneaten lunch. fragile fingers
snatch the meal away. saying nothing,
we depart with minor comforts.

Chuck Wemple

Anahuac Roundup

Alligator bigger than me
Bigger than a station wagon
So green he's almost black (almost)

How quickly he's pulled from the ground
Noose around his neck
The men are all too easy about this

Too eager to take your picture for a dollar
Right next to dangling feet
Slowly spinning above the crowd

Smaller gator
Dead on ice
Kids touch it prod it

A little girl   blonde ponytail
Gently places ice cubes on the gator's back
Hoping to keep him cool

She'll be fine

It's the son I worry about

The one who is crying
The one with the boozed up father
Hollering at him to put his head in the gator's mouth

Scott Wiggerman

Houston in the Cruelest Month

Starting with a Dickinson line (#168)

If the foolish call them flowers, need the wiser tell?
Is it a green thumb or a special fertilizer? Tell!

The hill leading down to the lake is sprinkled in primroses.
What somnambulant story does the tranquilizer tell?

Prairie coneflowers, sombreros thrusting up like sex.
O, tell how spring is the great naturalizer. Tell.

The park is awash in green abundance, high and low.
Good dirt runs out like good words, to hear the miser tell.

Yellow daisies sprouting up like jealousy, but whose?
The peach and plum daubed in pink—spring's appetizer—tell.

Indigo spires, bluebonnets, and phlox: a blue season.
How can a year alone be such a great reviser? Tell.

Someone planned this: the trees, the lakes, the fields of flowers.
Nature is not always natural. Tell, disguiser, tell.

Steve Wilson

Houston: On the Alligator

—days is teeth—teeth
and stone that's skin—

and an eye looking through

to the cash in the purse—
days is a black confession

gone buried for months

out back by the shed—where
the grass browns—already down

from this winter—or birds

hunker hard in bare trees
above the banks of the bayou—

days is days is what—

S.L. Wisenberg

Now We Know the Names

Lizards (green Carolina anoles), doodle bugs (sow bugs, pill bugs), huge whirring grasshoppers spitting their tobacco juice, dragonflies, squirrels, butterflies to catch in the net; beware of ant hills, mosquitoes, thorns, flies, bees, wasps, the hot pepper plant. (No, the plant was in the old house. So were the roses.) At the old house in the backyard I carried a heavy glass ashtray, collecting doodle bugs. There was green moss on the dirt but the only moss we knew was Spanish, bearding the trees. We walked along the bayou after the prom after he fell asleep (he said) and (I believed him) I sat on the couch waiting for him (the situation sadder than I felt).

What exactly was a bayou? They never said. Cement, water, logs. Pink buttercups, tall wheat-like grasses, trees of no particular species. (We didn't know species.) Once, a brown horse with a policeman on it, combing the lot behind us for a criminal. Empty lot. I didn't know the word suspect. If you grabbed a lizard by the tail, it would detach and the little reptile would run off. The tail would writhe on the ground. Scaring predators. Such as myself. But only the first time.

If you were lucky you'd see a lizard covered with a white veil of skin. Shedding. And you might see it take hold of that extra frosted-sheer coat with its little teeth and eat it. Everything was new but the bricks were a century old, older than our roots in Houston that went back only to the Depression. I wanted to go North. I do look back. I knew it was wrong to catch a live creature but I did and I did.

Vanessa Zimmer-Powell

Live Oak

On Flowerdale
the bulldozers were busy last night
taking Mrs. Miller's house,
her driveway,
the lake,
her neighbor's car.

This morning I walked into silence,
found a missing block of houses,
a devoured acre of sidewalk.

On this street the developers are hungry;
I feel their breath.
They send my house letters;
woo her in front of me.

She will get a new school,
fancy streets,
the drainage will be better.

I cast my eyes downward,
fear Stepford houses.
Am I strong enough?

Should I tell her that she will die
stripped of her trees and flattened
in just a few hours?

I think to send her a picture
of "Live Oak,"
the new neighborhood
within the neighborhood
whose acres
have only one live tree.

Biographies

Carolyn Adams' poetry, collage art, and photography have appeared in *Remarkable Doorways, Glass Mountain, San Pedro River Review, Mojave River Review,* and *Haunted Traveler,* among others. She has edited and co-edited the poetry publications *Curbside Review, Lily Literary Review, Ardent,* and *Mad Hatter's Review.* Her chapbooks are *Beautiful Strangers, What Do You See?, An Ocean of Names,* and *The Things You've Left Behind.* She was nominated for a Pushcart Prize and a finalist for the post of 2013 Houston Poet Laureate.

James Adams has studied creative writing and poetry at the University of Texas, UCLA, Oxford University, and l'Université Paris-Sorbonne (Paris IV). His poetry has appeared in several anthologies and reviews, including *The Muse* (India), *The David Jones Journal* (Wales), *The Pebblelake Review,* and *Five Inprint Poets.* His first poetry collection, *Noble Savage* (St. Lukes Presse), was nominated for a Pulitzer Prize. He served as lead editor for the critically acclaimed *Against Agamemnon: War Poetry 2009* (WaterWood Press) and is presently editing *No Achilles: War Poetry* (WaterWood Press).

Mike Alexander, a seed pod from New York City. Took root in Bayou City mud. Sheds leaves in & out of season.

Michael Baldwin is a native Texan who resided in the Houston area in the 1980s and 90s. He holds a B.A. in political science, and master's degrees in library science and public administration. He was a juried poet at the Houston Poetry Fest and has presented at the Austin International Poetry Festival, Langdon Literary Weekend, and Montgomery County Literary Arts Festival among others. His book, *Scapes*, won the Eakin Poetry Book Award in 2011, and his chapbook, *Counting Backward From Infinity*, won the Morris Memorial Award, 2012. He currently resides in Benbrook, Texas.

Joe Barnes' poetry has appeared in four anthologies—*TimeSlice, The Weight of Addition, Improbable Worlds* and *Lineup*—and in journals such as *Bat City Review, Measure,* and *Illya's Honey*. He is also a playwright and lives in Houston, Texas.

David A. Bart is a writer from Arlington, Texas. His poetry appears in the journals *Poet Lore, Sixfold, Borderlands: Texas Poetry Review, Margie, Cider Press Review, Illya's Honey, Red River Review* and *The Weight of Addition* (Mutabilis Press, Houston).

Kristi Beer lives in Houston with her daughter, two canines and five cats. Her goal in life is to sit at cafés, read, and write.

Paula Beltrán worked as court advocate and interpreter-translator in the greater Houston area prior to completing an M.F.A. in fiction from George Mason University, where she was the recipient of an honors award. An alumna of the VONA Voices Workshop, she serves on the editorial board of *So to Speak: a feminist journal of language and art*. Her work has appeared in the *Huffington Post, AOL Latino,* and the *Houston Press*.

Michael Berryhill is the chair of journalism at Texas Southern University. He has published two chapbooks of poetry, *Not Now* and *Everything Changes* (both from Inleaf Press). His poems have appeared in *The Paris Review, Western Humanities Review,* and most recently in the magazine *Consequences*.

Ann Reisfeld Boutté, a former writer for a national news service, has recent work in *Garden Blessings, Seek It, New Verse News,* and *Through a Distant Lens: Travel Poems*.

Barbara Ann Carle is a poet and personal essay writer. She was born and raised in New York City. In 2008 her poem, "The Battle," won the Ted O. Badger Award. Her book, *New York Rhapsody,* was published in 2009. Her poems have appeared in the *2010, 2011,* and *2012 Texas Poetry Calendars* and 2013 Spring *Rattle Magazine*. She is a member of Gulf Coast

Poets, Poetry Society of Texas, Spectrum Center Writers Guild, and Women in the Visual and Literary Arts. The mother of four and grandmother of six, she lives in Houston, Texas, with her husband Ed.

kathleen cook has lived in Houston all her adult life. It's a great city for poetry, innovation, and mischief of all sorts, and she has been a beneficiary of this gumbo.

Sara Cooper received her M.F.A. in poetry at New Mexico State University. Her writing has appeared in *Mid-American Review, BorderSenses*, and *Puerto del Sol*. A chapbook of poems, *Mis—*, was published in 2014 (Grandma Moses Press). She teaches writing in Houston with Writers in the Schools and at the University of Houston, where she is pursuing a Ph.D.

Sarah Cortez is a Councilor of the Texas Institute of Letters. An award-winning poet and editor, she has hundreds of poems, essays, and short stories published in magazines, journals, and anthologies.

Kay L. Cox, a visual artist and poet, is the winner of the 2008 Robert Clark Appreciation Award and a member of Spectrum Writers Guild, Gulf Coast Poets, The Poetry Society of Texas, and Women in the Visual and Literary Arts. Her poems have been published in several *Texas Poetry Calendars, Map of Austin, Sol Magazine, That Thing We Do,* and anthologies. She has a gypsy soul, loves skinny vanilla lattes, hates housework and panty hose.

Stan Crawford is an attorney and a poet living in Houston, Texas. His poems have been published in *The Comstock Review, Poet Lore, Borderlands: Texas Poetry Review, Illya's Honey,* and elsewhere. He has been nominated for a Pushcart Prize and selected as a juried poet in the Houston Poetry Fest.

Carolyn Dahl was the grand prize winner for her ekphrastic poem in the 2015 ART*lines*[2] Poetry Competition sponsored by the Museum of Fine

Arts, Houston and Public Poetry. She has also been a PEN Texas finalist award winner in nonfiction; had work in the anthologies *Goodbye, Mexico* (Texas Review Press), *Women On Poetry* (McFarland), and *Beyond Forgetting* (Kent State); and been published in the literary magazines *Colere, Copper Nickel, Camas,* and *Hawai'i Review*. Also an artist, she is the author of *Natural Impressions* and *Transforming Fabric*, and a co-author with Carolyn Florek of *The Painted Door Opened,* a book of poetry and art.

Robin Davidson is a poet, translator, and professor of literature and creative writing at the University of Houston-Downtown. She is author of two poem chapbooks, *Kneeling in the Dojo* and *City that Ripens on the Tree of the World*, and a full collection, *Luminous Other*. In 2003-4 she served as Fulbright professor of American literature at the Jagiellonian University in Kraków, Poland, and with Ewa Elżbieta Nowakowska, she translated a selection of Ewa Lipska's poems, *The New Century*. She serves on the editorial board of the American Literary Press, Calypso Editions, and in 2015, was named Houston's second Poet Laureate by Mayor Annise Parker.

Margo Davis is a recent Pushcart Prize nominee. Her poetry has appeared in *Midwest Quarterly Review, Slipstream, Agave Magazine, A Clean, Well-Lighted Place; Texas Poetry Calendar, Houston Poetry Festival,* and *Goodbye, Mexico*. When not working, she slips off to film festivals, where she reads poetry and foreign literature between screenings.

Diane DeGaetani started writing poetry at the age of twelve. As a child, she was very influenced by the Romantic poets and later by Zen poets and the Beats. She leans toward writing from an Eastern philosophical point of view. She edits and proofreads for a financial services company and formerly worked as a licensed massage therapist. She has been a featured reader at the Words & Art series at Rice University and her poetry has appeared in the *Bayou Review*. She is a native of Brooklyn, New York, and has lived in Houston since 2001.

Winston Derden is a poet, fiction writer, and former journalist. His poetry publications include *New Texas*, two Houston Poetry Fest anthologies, *Harbinger Asylum, Pink-Eye Lemonade, Big River Poetry Review, Illya's Honey, Just This*, and *Barbaric Yawp*. He is a Word Around Town veteran and a frequent headliner at Houston-area poetry readings. He also co-produces and hosts the reading/interview series Speak!Poet.

Carolyn Tourney Florek is a poet, publisher, garden designer, and visual artist, currently living in Santa Fe, New Mexico. She has a B.S. in geology (1977) from Wayne State University and a B.F.A. in painting from the University of Tulsa (1982). Her poetry has been published in *The Texas Review, Illya's Honey*, several Houston Poetry Fest anthologies, among other publications. Her poem, "Over Flat Creek," published in the *Texas Poetry Calendar 2014*, was nominated for a Pushcart Prize. She is co-founder with her husband, Bob, of Mutabilis Press, and is an artist-in-residence at Bandelier National Monument in late 2015.

Dede Fox's poetry has appeared in *di-vêrsé-city, The Enigmatist, Poetica, Sol, A Summer's Poems, Swirl*, and *Texas Poetry Calendar*. "Chapultepec Park" won the 2008 Christina Sergeyevna Award at the Austin International Poetry Festival, and she has twice been a juried poet at Houston Poetry Fest. Her poetry books include *Confessions of a Jewish Texan* (Poetica Press, May 2013) and *Postcards Home* (Ink Brush Press, August 2014). An educator, she taught with Houston's Writer in the Schools and serves on the board of the Montgomery County Literary Arts Council.

Priscilla Frake is the author of *Correspondence* (Mutabilis Press, 2013), a book of epistolary poems. She has published poetry in several anthologies and in dozens of journals, including *Nimrod, The Midwest Quarterly, Dark Matter, Crack the Spine*, and *The Sow's Ear Poetry Review*. Her honors include the Lorene Pouncey Award at the Houston Poetry Fest and a Pushcart nomination. She lives in Sugar Land, where she is a studio jeweler.

Adamarie Fuller's poems have appeared in numerous publications. She was a winner in the ART*lines* Poetry Competition in 2012, sponsored by the Museum of Fine Arts, Houston and Public Poetry, for her ekphrastic poem; voice recording is in the museum archives. She won honorable mention in the Austin International Poetry Festival 2011 and the *Texas Poetry Calendar 2009*. She has been published in several anthologies including *The Weight of Addition,* Austin International Poetry Festival Anthology *di-vêrsé-city* (2008 through 2012), *A Summer's Poems, The Poetry Revolt,* and *Poetry at Round Top,* as well as the Houston Poetry Fest anthologies (2009, 2011, 2012). She is a native Houstonian.

Jeannie Gambill's poetry has appeared in *Gulf Coast, Cenizo, The Weight of Addition,* and the *Texas Poetry Calendars* (2011 and 2012). She received the 2011 Dana Award for Poetry. She has been a featured poet in Houston's Public Poetry Library Reading Series, and she was a winner in the ART*lines* Poetry Competition in 2012, sponsored by the Museum of Fine Arts, Houston and Public Poetry, for her ekphrastic poem. She lives in Bellaire, Texas.

Elisa A. Garza has published two chapbooks, *Entre la Claridad* (Mouthfeel Press) and *Familia* (a bestseller for The Portlandia Group). Her poems have been awarded a literature fellowship from the Texas Commission on the Arts and the Emerging Writer Award from the Alfredo Cisneros del Moral Foundation. She has taught writing, literature, and women's studies courses in the community and at the university level. She currently works as a staff member at the University of Houston-Downtown and is editing her full-length manuscript.

John Gorman lives in Galveston where he leads the monthly working group Poets Roundtable. In 2014, he retired from the University of Houston-Clear Lake, having taught literature and creative writing there since its founding in 1974.

Maryann Gremillion has been as a writer-in-residence with Writers in the Schools for the past seven years. She's worked with teachers, the

Menil Collection, cancer patients, and Houston Grand Opera. In August 2015, she joined the staff at WITS as a program administrator. She has also facilitated writing workshops for women and coached students privately. Her work has appeared in *The Sun, Teachers & Writers, Telling Our Stories Press*, and MD Anderson's *Cancerwise*.

William Guest lives in Houston, Texas. His poems have appeared in poetry magazines, including *The New Lantern Review, Calliope, The Enigmatist, VOICES: A Journal of Poetry, Illya's Honey, Calliope, Blood & Thunder, Storyteller Magazine, Weight of Addition: an anthology of Texas Poetry*. He has also been a juried poet in the Houston Poetry Fest.

Laura Quinn Guidry's poems have been published in journals, including *The Texas Review, Concho River Review, descant* and *Louisiana Literature*, in the *San Antonio Express-News* and the *Texas Poetry Calendar*. Her work also appears in anthologies, including *The Weight of Addition* and *In These Latitudes: Ten Contemporary Poets*. She was a featured poet at Poetry on the Move in San Antonio in 2012. She grew up in New Orleans, lived in Houston for 30 years, and has retired to Carmine, Texas. She coordinates literary events at the Round Top Family Library.

Marian Haddad, Pushcart-nominated, wrote *Wildflower. Stone.* (Pecan Grove Press, 2011), which was endorsed by Yusef Komunyakaa: This collection "…celebrates the observable mysteries of daily existence … these poems have dropped all disguises, and each rides the pure joy of music. There are superb leaps and silences that deftly highlight the monumental in simple things." She has published *Saturn Falling Down* (2003) and a full-length collection, *Somewhere between Mexico and a River Called Home* (PecanGrove, 2004). Her poems, essays, reviews, and articles are published in journals, anthologies, and periodicals in the United States, Belgium, and the Middle East. Her poetry was referenced by Laura Bush in her book. She teaches creative writing.

Jerry Hamby teaches English and humanities at Lee College in Baytown, Texas. He has published in several literary journals and anthologies, including *The Texas Review, Concho River Review, New Texas, Windhover, Palo Alto Review, descant, CCTE Studies, Texas Poetry Calendar,* and *Lifting the Sky: Southwestern Haiku & Haiga*. His poetry collection is *Letters Drawn in Water* (Pecan Grove Press). He was a juried poet at Houston Poetry Fest 2010 and 2014 and a featured poet at Houston Poetry Fest 2011.

Michelle Hartman's work was recently featured in the *Langdon Review of the Arts*, and also appears in *Slipstream, Plainsongs, Carve, Crannog, Poetry Quarterly, The Pedestal Magazine, Raleigh Review, San Pedro River Review, Concho River Review*, and *RiverSedge*. Her work appears in multiple countries overseas. Her first book of poetry was *Disenchanted and Disgruntled* (Lamar University Press, available from Amazon). Her newest book is *Irony and Irreverence* (Lamar University Press, 2015). She is the editor for the online journal, *Red River Review*, and holds a B.S. in political science-pre-law from Texas Wesleyan University.

Bradley Earle Hoge is the managing editor of *Dark Matter: a journal of speculative literature*. His poems appear in numerous literary journals and anthologies, including *Chronogram, Rattle, Tertulia, Stickman Review, Tonapah la, entelechy: mind and culture*, and *Tar Wolf Review*. His most recent chapbook is *Clacking Things* (KattyWompus Press). He also has chapbooks published by Red Berry Editions and Plain View Press. He lives in Spring, Texas, with his wife and three children. He teaches natural science at the University of Houston-Downtown.

Adam Holt left a perfectly good teaching job to write full time. He publishes young adult science fiction and poetry. Other than that, he coaches volleyball every fall, travels when he has money, and loves the crunchy boom of a rocket launch.

Cindy Huyser's chapbook, *Burning Number Five: Power Plant Poems*, was selected co-winner of the 2014 Blue Horse Press Poetry Chapbook contest. Her poetry has appeared in a variety of publications, including *The Comstock Review, The Nassau Review, Borderlands: Texas Poetry Review, San Pedro River Review*, and *Layers* (Plain View Press, 1994). She co-edited the

Texas Poetry Calendar from 2009-2014 and has been a featured reader for Houston's Public Poetry Library Reading Series and the Houston Poetry Fest. She hosts a monthly poetry reading and open mic at BookWoman in Austin, Texas.

Angélique Jamail's poetry and essays have appeared in over two dozen anthologies and journals, including *Pluck* (2011), *The Milk of Female Kindness—An Anthology of Honest Motherhood* (2013), and *Waxwing* (2014). Her magic realism novella, *Finis.* (2014), has been praised by novelist Ari Marmell as having "some of the most real people I've encountered via text," and by poet Marie Marshall as "a witty tale of conformity, prejudice, and transformation, in a world that is disturbing as much for its familiarity as for its strangeness." She teaches creative writing and English.

Joshua C. Jones is a candidate for the M.F.A. at UMass Boston. His poetry has appeared in *The Mayo Review, Dappled Things,* and *Fourteen Hills*. He currently lives in Dorchester, Mass., with Lesleigh, his wonderfully nerdy wife, and their dog Guinevere.

Claire Kageyama-Ramakrishnan's first book, *Shadow Mountain,* won the Four Way Books Intro Book Prize, and was published by Four Way Books; her second book is *Bear, Diamonds and Crane* (Four Way Books, 2011). She is a full-time English instructor at Houston Community College in Houston, Texas, a graduate of the Ph.D. in literature and creative writing program at the University of Houston, where she was a Cambor Fellow. She lives in Houston with her husband, daughter, and three cats.

Laurence V. Kelly was born in 1940, San Francisco. Air Corps family moves brought 21 schools. Moved to Houston in 1964. Is now in semi-retirement as a real estate investor. Active in Chinese martial arts. Hobbies of music (playing the bass fiddle) and Chinese calligraphy. Writing poetry is not a choice for him, it comes unbidden. He has written poetry since his early 20s.

Jim LaVilla-Havelin is the author of four books of poetry, the most recent *Counting* (Pecan Grove Press, 2010). He is the San Antonio coordinator of National Poetry Month, poetry editor for the *San Antonio Express-News*, and a creative writing teacher for a variety of audiences through Gemini Ink, Bihl Haus Arts, and other sites.

Catherine Lee spent her early years on the East Coast but transplanted to central Texas over ten years ago. She is a high school teacher, wife, and mother who enjoys reading and playing with words. Her work has appeared in print and online publications, including *Red River Review, Poetry Quarterly, Wilderness House Journal, Poetic Bloomings, Impact: An Anthology of Short Memoirs*, and *Reverie Anthology*.

Thad Logan teaches in the English department at Rice University. She has written on Victorian material culture and has an M.F.A. from Warren Wilson College. Her poems have been published in previous Mutabilis Press anthologies. A native Houstonian, she escapes to West Virginia for the summer.

Janet Lowery's poetry has appeared in several literary reviews and anthologies. She has published a chapbook, *Thin Dimes* (Wings Press, 1992). Her trilogy of plays, *Traffic in Women*, was produced 2006-2008 at the University of St. Thomas, Houston, where she teaches full time in the English department. Odonata House published monologues from the plays in 2008. *A Heroine-Free Summer* will be produced by Mildred's Umbrella Theatre Company in Houston during the 2016-2017 season. She is a licensed massage therapist, a foundational practitioner of Reconnective Healing, and a consultant for the holistic nursing program at the University of St. Thomas.

Anne Robinson Mabry is a full-time, high school visual arts teacher and part-time poet living in Houston, Texas.

Dodie Messer Meeks has poetry in a couple of hundred literary publications, including *Antioch Review, Southwest Review,* and several editions of *Visions International* and *The Lyric,* the only poetry publisher older than she is. *Aloysius Alligator,* a picture book of children's poetry—intended to help adults, who read to children, stay awake until the kids doze off—is to be published shortly after her ninetieth birthday in 2015.

John Milkereit is from Chicago, but is currently a rotating equipment engineer working at an engineering contracting firm in Houston, Texas. His poems have appeared in various literary journals such as *Big River Poetry Review* and *San Pedro River Review.* His chapbooks are *Home & Away* and *Paying Admissions* (Pudding House Press, 2010). He is currently enrolled in the third year of a low-residency M.F.A. program in creative writing at the Rainier Writing Workshop in Tacoma, Wash. His new collection of poems is *A Rotating Equipment Engineer Is Never Finished* (Ink Brush Press, March 2015).

Terry Jude Miller is a poet from Houston. A juried poet for the 2011 and 2012 Houston Poetry Fests, his work has been published in scores of publications, including the *Texas Poetry Calendar, Harbinger Asylum,* the University of Houston's *Bayou Review, Ancient Paths, Orbis, Stepping Stones Magazine, Furnace Review, Shine Journal, Live Oak Review, Foundling Review, Houston Literary Review, Boston Literary Magazine,* the *Edison Literary Review,* and the *Birmingham Arts Journal.* His books of poetry are *The Day I Killed Superman, What If I Find Only Moonlight?,* and *The Butterfly Canonical.* He is the creator of the Texas Poets Podcast.

Jane E. Mulholland writes poetry when the muse speaks. More often she prefers to write personal essays, although her poems definitely reflect her experience. She came to Houston in 1982 when the department of the oil company she worked for was transferred to the city. She asked, "Does Houston have an opera company?" When the answer was affirmative, she agreed to move. Through Women in the Visual and Literary Arts, she has discovered Houston's vibrant and lively arts scene.

Mark Stephen Mullee was born in Houston and studied creative writing at the University of Houston. He currently lives in Rotterdam, The Netherlands, which is also Europe's largest port, a city with its own weird mix of industry and nature.

Carol Louise Munn lives in Houston and teaches English at Awty International School. Her poems have appeared in many journals and anthologies, including *Poetry, The GSU Review, Fugue, WomenArts Quarterly Journal,* and *Poetry Quarterly*. She won an Academy of American Poets Prize and was a finalist in the Atlanta Review International Poetry Competition.

Sheryl L. Nelms is from Marysville, Kansas, and graduated from South Dakota State University. She has had over 5,000 articles, stories and poems published, including fourteen individual collections of her poems. She is the fiction/nonfiction editor of *The Pen Woman Magazine*, the National League of American Pen Women publication, a contributing editor for *Time Of Singing, A Magazine Of Christian Poetry* and a three time Pushcart Prize nominee.

Stella Nesanovich is the author of four chapbooks of poems: *A Brightness That Made My Soul Tremble: Poems on the Life of Hildegard of Bingen, My Mother's Breath, My Father's Voice,* and *Dance, O, Heart, Double Round: Poems on Mechthild of Magdeburg* as well as a full-length collection, *Vespers at Mount Angel*. She is professor emerita of English from McNeese State University in Lake Charles, La.

David Olsen, formerly employed in Shell's Houston head office, is now a professional poet and playwright. *Unfolding Origami* (2015) won the Cinnamon Press Poetry Collection Award for full-length books. Poetry chapbooks from American publishers include *Sailing to Atlantis* (2013), *New World Elegies* (2011), and *Greatest Hits* (2001). His work has appeared in dozens of journals and anthologies on both sides of the Atlantic. He holds a B.A. in chemistry from University of California, Berkeley and an M.A. in creative writing from San Francisco State University.

Trilla Pando, a native Texan, lives and writes in Houston. Born in Amarillo, she still longs for the Panhandle sunsets while she relishes city life. Once an economics professor and newspaper columnist, she now writes whatever enters her head—especially poetry.

Mary Parham holds a Ph.D. in Latin American literature. A former professor of Spanish, she has been awarded two Fulbright Research Grants. Her poetry has been published by Naomi Shihab Nye in *The Texas Observer* and by Martha Serpas in the Mutabilis Press anthology *Improbable Worlds*. Her creative work has also appeared in *Ventanas Abiertas* (in Spanish) and in *The Caribbean Writer, Calyx, Poet Lore, The New Ohio Review* and many other journals and anthologies in the United States and Latin America.

Richard H. Peake published early poems in *Impetus* and the *Georgia Review*. Collections of his poems include *Wings Across …* and *Poems for Terence* (Vision Press), *Birds and Other Beasts*, and *Earth and Stars*. Recent poems have appeared in *Avocet, Jimson Weed, Red River Review*, and *The Anglican Theological Review*.

Donna E. Perkins is a visual artist and occasional writer of poems and plays. She is co-founder and current facilitator of The Archway Readings that began in 1997. These monthly readings are held at Archway Gallery in Houston, Texas.

Elina Petrova grew up and worked as an engineer in Ukraine. She has numerous Russian and Ukrainian publication credits, and a book of Russian-language poems. Since she moved to Texas in 2007, she has became a certified paralegal. She is a frequent featured reader in the Words & Art program at Rice University, and her poetry has been published in *Illya's Honey, FreeFall, Harbinger Asylum, Texas Poetry Calendar*, and the annual anthologies of the Houston and Austin poetry festivals. She has been nominated for the Pushcart Prize. Publication of her first book of poetry in English, *Aching Miracle*, is pending.

Dustin Pickering is founder of Transcendent Zero Press, a Houston-based poetry publisher. Transcendent Zero Press publishes the literary quarterly *Harbinger Asylum*. He has been published in *Beatest State in the Union, Vagabonds: Anthology of the Mad Ones*, and several other publications.

henry 7. reneau, jr. writes words in fire to wake the world ablaze: free verse illuminated by courage that empathizes with all the awful moments, launching a freight train warning that blazes from the heart, like a chambered bullet exploding inadvertently. His poetry collection is *freedomland blues* (Transcendent Zero Press, September 2014). He also has an e-chapbook, *physiography of the fittest* (Kind of a Hurricane Press, December 2014).

Lynn C. Reynolds is a past member of the Houston Poetry Society, the Texas Poetry Society, and Poets, Ink. She read at the Houston Poetry Fest in 1982, 1985, and 2012. She is published in *From Hide and Horn, a Sesquicentennial Anthology of Texas Poets* (Eakin Press, 1985).

Sally Ridgway is a longtime Houstonian whose poetry has been published in Texas anthologies, including *Big Land, Big Sky, Big Hair* and *Improbable Worlds* and in literary journals, including *Gulf Coast, The Texas Review,* and the newspaper *The Texas Observer*. She has taught creative writing through Writers in the Schools and The Jung Center, and English at high schools in Galveston and Houston, and at Houston Community College. She has an M.F.A. in writing from Vermont College.

Gary S. Rosin is a poet and photographer. His poems and short stories have appeared, or are forthcoming, in various literary and poetry magazines and anthologies, including *Harbinger Asylum, Lifting the Sky: Southwestern Haiku and Haiga, Texas Poetry Calendar* (2012, 2013, and 2014), and *Visions International*. He is the author of the chapbooks, *Standing Inside the Web* (Bear House Publishing, 1990), which won the 1990 Lucidity Chapbook Contest, and *Fire and Shadows* (The Legal Studies Forum, 2008). Selections of his poetry and photography can be found on his website, 4P Creations. He is the program chair of the Houston Poetry Fest.

Varsha Saraiya-Shah is an Indian-American, a poet, and former financial professional. She lives and works in Houston, Texas. Her work has appeared in *Asian Cha, Borderlands: Texas Poetry Review, Convergence,* Mutabilis Press anthologies, including *Five Inprint Poets, Texas Observer,* University of Texas Press book of *Photography & Poetry,* and elsewhere. She reads her new work regularly among multi-genre writers at Archway Gallery and ekphrastic poetry at Rice Gallery, invited and inspired by new installations.

Jenna Pashley Smith, born and raised in Indiana, can't remember a time when she didn't play with words. After dabbling in a variety of jobs, including carnival sideshow worker, toilet bowl cleaning professional, annoying telemarketer, musician, and researcher of Angolan artifacts, she gave up all attempts to define herself as anything other than a writer. She currently lives in Houston, Texas.

Loueva Smith is a poet and playwright. Her writing has appeared in several journals and anthologies, and her plays have been presented at FrenetiCore Theater in Houston.

Rebecca A. Spears, a poet and instructor from Houston, Texas, is the author of *The Bright Obvious* (Finishing Line Press). Her poems and essays have appeared in *TriQuarterly, Calyx, Crazyhorse, Ars Medica, Minnesota Review, Nimrod, Relief, Borderlands: Texas Poetry Review*, and other journals and anthologies. She has received awards from the Taos Writers Workshop, Vermont Studio Center, and The Writers Colony at Dairy Hollow. She recently received a Pushcart nomination.

Sandi Stromberg worked for many years as a professional editor and magazine feature writer, with hundreds of publications in both the United States and Europe. Her poetry has been nominated for a Pushcart Prize and appeared in eight Houston Poetry Fest anthologies. She has also published in *Borderlands: Texas Poetry Review, Red River Review, Illya's Honey, Texas Poetry Calendar, Colere*, among others, and in anthologies: *TimeSlice, The Weight of Addition*, and *Improbable Worlds* from Mutabilis Press, *Crossing Lines* from Main Street Rag, and *Goodbye, Mexico* from Texas Review Press.

Larry D. Thomas, a member of the Texas Institute of Letters, served as the 2008 Texas Poet Laureate. He has published several collections of poetry, the most recent of which is *As If Light Actually Matters: New & Selected Poems* (Texas Review Press, Member, Texas A&M University Press Consortium). Among his many honors and awards are two Texas Review Poetry Prizes, two Western Heritage Awards (Western Heritage Museum, Oklahoma City, Okla.), the Violet Crown Book Award (Writers' League of Texas), nomination for the 2007 Poets' Prize (Nicholas Roerich Museum), and six Pushcart Prize nominations.

Nancy Thorleifson is a retired educator residing in Katy, Texas. Her work has appeared in Houston Poetry Fest anthologies and will be included in *ARTlines²* forthcoming ekphrastic anthology sponsored by the Museum of Fine Arts, Houston and Public Poetry.

Margo Stutts Toombs is a writer, performance artist, internal humorist, and filmmaker. Her poetry has been published in the 2011 *Texas Poetry Calendar; Love over 60: An Anthology of Women's Poems,* and Archway Gallery anniversary chapbooks.

Elizabeth Tornes has published two chapbooks, *New Moon* (Finishing Line Press, 2013) and *Snowbound* (Giiwedin Press, 2011), and been first prize winner of the 2012 Wisconsin Fellowship of Poets Chapbook Contest. Her poems have been published widely in literary journals, including *Antioch Review, bornmagazine.com, Boulevard, Durak, Field, Gulf Coast, Main Street Rag, Missouri Review, The New American Review, The New Republic, Ploughshares, Southern Review, Verse Wisconsin,* and *Western Humanities Review.* She holds a Ph.D. in creative writing from the University of Utah. She has also published a collection of Ojibwe oral histories, *Memories of Lac du Flambeau Elders* (University of Wisconsin Press, 2004).

William Turner is a retired geologist and enjoys writing poetry. His poetry has appeared in *The Weight of Addition*, and in several online publications, including *Sol Magazine*.

Evangelina Vigil is a nationally recognized poet and the recipient of prestigious literary awards. She is the author of several books of poetry and a children's book published by Arte Publico Press. She also is translator of the literary classic *Y No Se Lo Tragó la Tierra/And the Earth Did Not Devour Him* by Tomás Rivera and editor of the first anthology of U.S. Latina literature. She holds the post of public information officer with the City of Houston and is a longtime adjunct lecturer at the University of Houston, where she teaches U.S. Hispanic literature.

Randall Watson's *The Sleep Accusations* received the Blue Lynx Poetry Award at Eastern Washington University and is currently available through Carnegie Mellon University Press. His first book, *Las Delaciones del Sueño*, was published in a bi-lingual edition by the Universidad Veracruzana in Xalapa, Mexico. His novella, *Petals,* (under the pseudonym Ellis Reece) won the Quarterly West Novella Competition.

Weasel is a writer and overall degenerate poet. He received his B.A. in literature at the University of Houston-Clear Lake, and started Weasel Press. The vagabond poet has released a full-length poetry collection, *Ashes to Burn* (Transcendent Zero Press). His writing has been accepted in several publications, including Houston's *Harbinger Asylum, Threshold, Permian Basin Beyond 2014, Hunger For Peace, Everything on Earth is Huge and We're All On It,* and *di-vêrsé-city*. He also appeared in a small documentary about art, "Something Out of Nothing (S.O.O.N)," directed by Mitchell Dudley.

Chuck Wemple is a scientist and poet currently living and working in Houston, Texas. His interest in poetry began when he enrolled in a creative writing class at the University of Montana. An elective course at the end of his senior year, an afterthought at the time, the class has heavily influenced his life. He has written poetry for more than twenty-eight years; served as co-editor of the poetry review *Spiky Palm*; met his wife Mary at a poetry reading; and is currently exploring the world of executive management. His poetry incorporates themes of mythology, magical realism, and occasional circus bears.

Scott Wiggerman is the author of three books of poetry, *Leaf and Beak: Sonnets*, *Presence*, and *Vegetables and Other Relationships*; and the editor of several volumes, including *Wingbeats: Exercises & Practice in Poetry*, *Lifting the Sky: Southwestern Haiku & Haiga*, and *Wingbeats II*. Recent poems have appeared in *Naugatuck River Review*, *Frogpond*, *Pinyon Review*, *Borderlands: Texas Poetry Review*, and the anthologies *This Assignment Is So Gay*, *Pushing the Envelope* and *The Queer South*. He is chief editor for Dos Gatos Press, now of Albuquerque, New Mexico.

Steve Wilson, who teaches at Texas State University, has poems in journals and anthologies nationwide. His most recent book is *The Lost Seventh*. His work also appeared in the recent Mutabilis anthology, *Improbable Worlds*.

S.L. Wisenberg was born in St. Joseph Hospital, which was segregated at the time. Schools: Beth Yeshurun, Longfellow, Johnston, Bellaire. Jobs: Astroworld, Houston West Side Reporter. Books: *The Sweetheart Is In* (Northwestern University Press); *Holocaust Girls: History, Memory & Other Obsessions* (Nebraska); *The Adventures of Cancer Bitch* (Iowa); and *Moments in Selma & Other Glimpses of the South* (with more Jews than you would think), forthcoming in fall 2015 from University of Georgia Press. She lives in Chicago.

Vanessa Zimmer-Powell is a member of Houston's Poets in The Loop. She is frequently featured at the Rice Gallery Words & Art Reading Series, the Friendswood Public Library Reading Series, and has been a featured reader at the Houston First Friday Reading Series. She has been interviewed by Catherine Lu of Houston Public Media for her ekphrastic poetry and was the winner of a Rick Steve's Haiku Award. Her poetry has been published in the *The Avocet*, the *Austin International Poetry Fest Anthology*, *Blue Hole*, *Ekphrasis*, *the Houston Poetry Fest Anthology*, *Harbinger Asylum*, and the *Texas Poetry Calendar*.

Mutabilis Press is a non-profit literary press dedicated to the publication of poetry, with focus on writers living or working in Houston and the surrounding area.

◆ ◆ ◆

Also published by Mutabilis Press:

TimeSlice: Houston Poetry 2005

The Weight of Addition: an Anthology of Texas Poetry (2007)
Randall Watson, editor

Why Me? (2009)
Rich Levy

Some Recognition of the Joshua Lizard (2009)
Robert Burlingame

Improbable Worlds: an anthology of Texas and Louisiana Poets (2011)
Martha Serpas, editor

Isthmus (2013)
Daniel Rifenburgh

Correspondence (2013)
Priscilla Frake

◆ ◆ ◆

For more information, see **www.mutabilispress.org**